The Royal Court Theatre
presents

Harry and Me

by Nigel Williams

ff

faber and faber
LONDON · BOSTON

First performed at the Royal Court Theatre on 21 March 1996.

The Royal Court Theatre presents this production
by arrangement with the Theatre of Comedy Company Ltd.

PRUDENTIAL AWARDS
FOR THE ARTS

1995

The Royal Court Theatre is financially assisted by the
Royal Borough of Kensington and Chelsea.
Recipient of a grant from the Theatre Restoration Fund
& from the Foundation for Sport & the Arts.
The Royal Court's Play Development Programme is
funded by the Audrey Skirball-Kenis Theatre.
The Royal Court Registered Charity number 231242

first call
TICKETS · 24 HOURS
0171 420 0100

FUNDED BY
LONDON
BOROUGHS
GRANTS
COMMITTEE

Funded by
THE
ARTS
COUNCIL
OF ENGLAND

The creation of a *Theatre of Comedy* was, for many years, the cherished ambition of Ray Cooney. He knew that this country possessed some of the finest comedy writers, directors and performers in the world and the founding of a Theatre of Comedy was long overdue. His ideas met with enthusiastic responses within the theatrical profession and the company was formed. It included as Founder Members of the company some 30 outstanding figures from the world of British Comedy, all of whom were prepared to give not only their names and talents, but their time and energy to the creation and maintaining of a Theatre of Comedy Company.

The numerous highly successful productions presented by the Theatre of Comedy include **Run For Your Wife** in 1983, Peter O'Toole in **Pygmalion**, the late Leonard Rossiter in **Loot**, Peter Nichols' **Passion Play**, Alan Ayckbourn's **Intimate Exchanges**, Donald Sinden and Michael Williams in **Two Into One** and all-star revivals of **See How They Run**, **Rookery Nook**, **When We Are Married** (Olivier award-winning production, 1986) and Ray Cooney's **Out Of Order** (Olivier Award for Best Comedy 1990). The company owns the Shaftesbury Theatre which has been, with great care, both restored to its former Edwardian glory and modernised to the exacting technical demands of a theatre today. The hit musical **Tommy** has just started its run.

The company also produced **Pocket Dream**, with Mike McShane and Sandi Toksvig at the Albery Theatre, co-produced the Olivier award-winning **Six Degrees of Separation** (with the *Royal Court*) and **June Moon** (with *Hampstead Theatre*) and produced Coward's **Hay Fever** with Maria Aitken and John Standing at the Albery Theatre. John Godbur's **Happy Families** was co-produced with *Hull Truck* and Terry Johnson's **Hysteria** (co-produced with the *Royal Court*) was winner of the 1994 Olivier award for Comedy of the Year. A revival of **The Prime of Miss Jean Brodie** starring Patricia Hodge was produced at the Strand Theatre. Recently the Company took over the management of the Churchill Theatre, Bromley and **Hot Mikado** transferred from there to the Queen's Theatre. The Company has continued its association with Royal Court by co-producing the Classics Season at the Duke of York's Theatre.

The Company co-produces the very popular TV series **As Time Goes By** starring Founder-Members Dame Judi Dench and Geoffrey Palmer. The Company also co-produced a four part series **Love on a Branch Line**, adapted by David Nobbs from the novel by John Hadfield.

For the Theatre of Comedy Company

Alan Strachan Artistic Director
Andrew Welch Chief Executive
Graham Cowley Co-Executive
Don Taffner Chairman

How the Royal Court is Brought to you

The English Stage Company at the Royal Court Theatre is supported financially by a wide range of public bodies and private companies, as well as its own trading activities. The theatre receives its principal funding from the **Arts Council of England**, which has supported the Royal Court since 1956. The **Royal Borough of Kensington & Chelsea** gives an annual grant to the Royal Court Young People's Theatre and provides some of its staff. The **London Boroughs Grants Committee** contributes to the cost of productions in the Theatre Upstairs.

Other parts of the Royal Court's activities are made possible by business sponsorships. Several of these sponsors have made a long-term commitment. 1996 will see the sixth Barclays New Stages Festival of Independent Theatre, supported throughout by **Barclays Bank**. **British Gas North Thames** supported three years of the Royal Court's Education Programme. Sponsorship by **WH Smith** helped to make the launch of the Friends of the Royal Court scheme so successful.

1993 saw the start of our association with the **Audrey Skirball-Kenis Theatre**, of Los Angeles. The Skirball Foundation is funding a Playwrights Programme at the Royal Court. Exchange visits for writers between Britain and the USA complement the greatly increased programme of readings and workshops which have fortified the Royal Court's capability to develop new plays.

In 1988 the Royal Court launched the **Olivier Building Appeal** to raise funds to begin the task of restoring, repairing and improving the theatre building, made possible by a large number of generous supporters and significant contributions from the **Theatres Restoration Fund**, the **Rayne Foundation**, the **Foundation for Sport and the Arts** and the **Arts Councils Incentive Funding Scheme**.

The Royal Court earns the rest of the money it needs to operate from the Box Office, from other trading and from the transfers of plays such as **Death and the Maiden**, **Six Degrees of Separation**, **Oleanna** and **My Night With Reg** to the West End. But without public subsidy it would close immediately and its unique place in British Theatre would be lost. If you care about the future of arts in this country, please write to your MP and say so.

The English Stage Company at The Royal Court Theatre

The English Stage Company was formed to bring serious writing back to the stage. The Court's first Artistic Director, George Devine, wanted to create a vital and popular theatre. He encouraged new writing that explored subjects drawn from contemporary life as well as pursuing European plays and forgotten classics. When John Osborne's **Look Back in Anger** was first produced in 1956, it forced British Theatre into the modern age. But, the Court was much more than a home for *'Angry Young Men'* illustrated by a repertoire that ranged from Brecht to Ionesco, by way of J P Sartre, Marguerite Duras, Wedekind and Beckett.

The ambition was to discover new work which was challenging, innovative and also of the highest quality, underpinned by the desire to discover a truly contemporary style of presentation. Early Court writers included Arnold Wesker, John Arden, David Storey, Ann Jellicoe, N F Simpson and Edward Bond. They were followed by a generation of writers led by David Hare and Howard Brenton, and in more recent years, celebrated house writers have included Caryl Churchill, Timberlake Wertenbaker, Robert Holman and Jim Cartwright. Many of their plays are now regarded as modern classics.

Since 1994 the Theatre Upstairs has programmed a major season of plays by writers new to the Royal Court, many of them first plays, produced in association with the *Royal National Theatre Studio* with sponsorship from *The Jerwood Foundation*. The writers included Joe Penhall, Nick Grosso, Judy Upton, Sarah Kane, Michael Wynne, Judith Johnson, James Stock and Simon Block.

Many established playwrights had their early plays produced in the Theatre Upstairs including Anne Devlin, Andrea Dunbar, Sarah Daniels, Jim Cartwright, Clare McIntyre, Winsome Pinnock, and more recently Martin Crimp and Phyllis Nagy.

Theatre Upstairs productions have regularly transferred to the Theatre Downstairs, as with Ariel Dorfman's **Death and the Maiden**, and last autumn Sebastian Barry's **The Steward of Christendom**, a co-production with *Out of Joint*.

1992-1995 have been record-breaking years at the box-office with capacity houses for productions of **Faith Healer**, **Death and the Maiden**, **Six Degrees of Separation**, **King Lear**, **Oleanna**, **Hysteria**, **Cavalcaders**, **The Kitchen**, **The Queen & I**, **The Libertine**, **Simpatico**, **Mojo** and **The Steward of Christendom**.

Death and the Maiden and **Six Degrees of Separation** won the Olivier Award for Best Play in 1992 and 1993 respectively. **Hysteria** won the 1994 Olivier Award for Best Comedy, and also the Writers' Guild Award for Best West End Play. **My Night with Reg** won the 1994 Writers' Guild Award for Best Fringe Play, the Evening Standard Award for Best Comedy, and Best Comedy 1994 Olivier Awards. Jonathan Harvey won the 1994 Evening Standard Drama Award for Most Promising Playwright, for **Babies**. Sebastian Barry won the 1995 Writers' Guild Award for Best Fringe Play for **The Steward of Christendom**, Jez Butterworth was named New Writer of the Year for **Mojo** by the Writers' Guild, won the Evening Standard Award for Most Promising Newcomer 1995 and the 1996 Olivier Award for Best Comedy. Phyllis Nagy won the 1995 Writers' Guild Award for Best Regional Play for **Disappeared**. The Royal Court was the overall winner of the 1995 Prudential Award for the Arts for creativity, excellence, innovation and accessibility, and the 1995 Peter Brook Empty Space Award for innovation and excellence in theatre.

Donal McCann in Sebastian Barry's **The Steward of Christendom**

Photo: John Haynes

After nearly four decades, the Royal Court's aims remain consistent with those established by George Devine. The Royal Court Theatre is still a major focus in the country for the production of new work. Scores of plays first seen in Sloane Square are now part of the national and international dramatic repertoire.

make sure you stay in touch

stay in touch with the freshest new plays and playwrights all year round.

mailing list

Join the Royal Court mailing list and you will receive:

* Regular advance mailings on all Royal Court activities at your home address.

* Occasional special offers

* Annual Cost: £5

Royal Court Friends

Become a friend of The Royal Court and you will be able to:

* Receive regular advance mailings on all Royal Court activities at your home address.

* Buy two top price seats to every production at the Royal Court for only £5 each.

* Take advantage of a priority booking period for each season.

* Attend play readings and other special events for free.

* Receive a newsletter containing behind the scenes information, in-depth analysis, fascinating insights into the workings of one of Europe's most exciting theatres, and special offers for anything from shows around town to exhibitions and hotel room prices..

* **Annual Cost: £15**   *(£25 initial joining fee)*

KEEP ON KEEPING IN TOUCH - JOIN BY TELEPHONE TODAY

CALL THE ROYAL COURT BOX OFFICE ON 0171 730 1745 TO START YOUR MEMBERSHIP

Harry and Me

by Nigel Williams

Cast *in alphabetical order*

RAY	**Ron Cook**
TRACY	**Sheila Hancock**
HARRY	**Dudley Sutton**

Director	James Macdonald
Designer	Tim Hatley
Lighting Designer	Johanna Town
Sound Designer	Paul Arditti
Stage Manager	Martin Christopher
Deputy Stage Manager	Julia Hendry
Assistant Stage Manager	Paul Anders
Student ASM	Victoria Garden
Costume Supervisor	Glenda Nash
Voice Coach	Joan Washington
Set constructed by	Stage Surgeons

The Royal Court Theatre are grateful to the following for their support of this production:
Hello Magazine, Braun (UK) Ltd. for coffee machine; Viking Direct for office furniture; Associated Newspapers for the Daily Mail; London Central Communications for the fax machine;Derek Reid at BT Archive; Dimplex (U.K) for convector heater; Oyez Stationery Group for office stationery; The Carphone Warehouse for mobile phones; Wye Water Company for water cooler; Betacom PLC for Answer machine; Woolworth PLC for binders; NEC (UK) Ltd.; Jet Stationery for box files; Brewhurst Health Food Supplies for menthol cigarettes; Dolland and Aitchison for spectacles; British Telecom for the telephones; Wardrobe care by Persil and Comfort courtesy of Lever Brothers Ltd, watches by The Timex Corporation, refrigerators by Electrolux and Philips Major Appliances Ltd.; kettles for rehearsals by Morphy Richards; video for casting purposes by Hitachi; backstage coffee machine by West 9; furniture by Knoll International; freezer for backstage use supplied by Zanussi Ltd 'Now that's a good idea.' Hair by Rick Strickland; Closed circuit TV cameras and monitors by Mitsubishi UK Ltd. Natural spring water from Wye Spring Water, 149 Sloane Street, London SW1, tel. 0171-730 6977. Overhead projector from W.H. Smith; Sanyo U.K for the backstage microwave; Sodastream.

NIGEL WILLIAMS *(writer)*

For the Royal Court: Class Enemy (Plays and Players Most Promising Playwright Award), Sugar and Spice.

Other plays include: Double Talk (Square One Theatre); Trial Run (Oxford Playhouse); Line Em (RNT); WCPC (Half Moon); My Brother's Keeper (Greenwich); Country Dancing (RSC Stratford); Lord of the Flies, an adaptation of the novel by William Golding (RSC); Nativity (Tricycle).

For television and film: Talking Blues, Real Live Audience, Baby Love, Johnny Jarvis, Charlie, BreakingUp, Kremlin Farewell, Centrepoint; The Last Romantics, Witchcraft, Skallagrigg (winner BAFTA Award), The Canterville Ghost, The Wimbledon Poisoner. Novels: My Life Closed Twice (winner, Somerset Maugham Award), Jack Be Nimble, Star Turn, Black Magic, Witchcraft, The Wimbledon Poisoner, They Came From SW19, East of Wimbledon, Two and a Half Men in a Boat, Scenes from a Poisoner's Life, From Wimbledon to Waco.

PAUL ARDITTI *(sound designer)*

For the Royal Court work includes: Sweetheart, Bruises, Pale Horse, The Changing Room, Hysteria, Rat in the Skull (Royal Court Classics), The Steward of Christendom (and Out of Joint), Mojo, Simpatico, The Strip, The Knocky, Blasted, Peaches, Some Voices, Thyestes, My Night with Reg, The Kitchen, Live Like Pigs, Search and Destroy.

Other theatre sound design includes: Tartuffe (Manchester Royal Exchange) The Threepenny Opera (Donmar Warehouse); Hamlet (Gielgud); Piaf (Piccadilly); St. Joan (Strand & Sydney Opera House); The Winter's Tale, Cymbeline, The Tempest, Antony & Cleopatra, The Trackers of Oxyrhynchus (Royal National Theatre); The Gift of the Gorgon (RSC & Wyndhams); Orpheus Descending (Theatre Royal, Haymarket & Broadway); The Merchant of Venice (Phoenix & Broadway); A Streetcar Named Desire (Bristol Old Vic); The Winter's Tale (Manchester Royal Exchange); The Wild Duck (Phoenix); Henry IV, The Ride Down Mount Morgan (Wyndhams); Born Again (Chichester); Three Sisters, Matador (Queens); Twelfth Night, The Rose Tattoo

(Playhouse); Two Gentlemen of Verona, Becket, Cyrano de Bergerac (Theatre Royal, Haymarket); Travesties (Savoy); Four Baboons Adoring the Sun (Lincoln Center, 1992 Drama Desk Award).

Opera includes: Gawain, Arianna (ROH); The Death of Moses (Royal Albert Hall). TV includes: The Camomile Lawn.

RON COOK

For the Royal Court: Faith Healer, Our Country's Good, The Recruiting Officer, Greenland, The Grass Widow, Cloud Nine, The Arbor.

Other theatre includes: The Machine Wreckers, Black Snow (RNT); Slavs, How I Got That Story, Loose Ends, Ecstasy (Hampstead); Glengarry Glen Ross (Donmar Warehouse); A Jovial Crew, Odyssey, The Merry Wives of Windsor, Mary After The Queen, The Crucible, The Winter's Tale, The Dillen, Television Times, The Irish Play, Henry VI, 'Tis Pity She's A Whore, Sons of Light (RSC); Vanilla (West End & tour); Cock Ups (Royal Exchange); She Stoops to Conquer (Lyric Hammersmith);Quantrille in Lawrence (ICA Foco Novo).

Television includes: Bramwell, The Singing Detective, Bergerac, The Miser, A Day to Remember, Richard III, Henry VI Part's I, II & II, The Merry Wives of Windsor, The Bill, Maigret, The Chief, The Boys from the Bush, The Detectives, Sharpe's Rifles, The Young Ones, Blackadder, Life of Will Shakespeare, Howay the Lads, The Stars Look Down, Girls on Top, Whoops Apocolypse, Boon.

Film includes: Secrets and Lies, The Fool, The Cook, The Thief, His Wife and Her Lover, Turbulence, Number One, The Magic Shop. Radio includes: Money, Faith Healer, The Merchant of Venice, Three Men in a Boat, Roads to Freedom.

SHEILA HANCOCK

For the Royal Court: The Soldier's Fortune, Fill the Stage with Happy Hours, Greenland. Recent theatre includes: The Cherry Orchard (RNT); Gypsy (West Yorkshire Playhouse); The Way of the World, Prin, Judgement in Stone (Lyric Hammersmith & West End).
Recent television includes:The Buccaneers, Dangerous Lady.
As director: Associate Director of Cambridge Arts Theatre; Artistic Director of RSC Tour; The Critic (RNT).
Author of Ramblings of an Actress.

TIM HATLEY (designer)

Recent design for theatre includes: Stanley (RNT) Days (Gate Dublin/Lincoln Center NY); The Three Lives Of Lucie Cabrol (Theatre de Complicite);Out of a House Walked a Man (RNT/Theatre de Complicite); The Nose (Nottingham Playhouse); Moscow Stations (Traverse/West End/Broadway); Reader (Traverse); Poor Superman (Traverse/Hampstead); Chatsky (Almeida); Richard III (RSC); The Misunderstanding, Damned for Despair (Gate).
Recent design for opera includes: Orpheus in the Underworld, The Return of Ulysses (Opera North); Il Trovatore (Scottish Opera); HMS Pinafore, Die Fledermaus (D'Oyly Carte Opera).
Recent design for ballet includes: Roughcut (Rambert Dance Company); Cinderella (Northern Ballet Theatre).
He won the Linbury Prize for Stage Design Dance Commission in 1989, the Plays & Players Best Designer 1991, a 1992 Time Out Award, and represented Britain at the Prague Quadrennial Exhibition of Theatre Design 1995 with the designs for The Three Lives of Lucie Cabrol (Theatre de Complicite).

JAMES MACDONALD (director)

For the Royal Court: The Changing Room (Royal Court Classics), Simpatico, Blasted, Peaches, Thyestes, The Terrible Voice of Satan, Hammett's Apprentice, Putting Two and Two Together.
Other theatre includes: Love's Labour's Lost, Richard II (Manchester Royal Exchange) Oedipus Rex (Royal Exchange/Halle); The Rivals (Nottingham Playhouse); The Crackwalker (Gate); The Seagull (Sheffield Crucible); Neon Gravy (RNT Studio); Miss Julie (Oldham Coliseum); Juno and the Paycock, Ice Cream & Hot Fudge, Romeo and Juliet, Fool for Love and Savage/Love, Master Harold & the Boys (Contact Theatre); Lives of the Great Poisoners (Second Stride, Riverside); Prem (BAC, Soho Poly); Good Person of Szechwan, The Dragon (I Gelati Theatre Company).

DUDLEY SUTTON

For the Royal Court: OGodilefthegason, Curse of the Starving Class.
Other Theatre includes: Strictly Entre Nous (BAC); Hangover Square (Lyric Hammersmith); Volpone (Edinburgh).
Television includes: Delta Force, Moses, Lovejoy, 1996, The Beiderbecke Affair, Widows, Juno and the Paycock.
Films include: Orlando, Edward II, Lamb, Valentino, Fellini's Casanova.

JOHANNA TOWN (lighting designer)

For the Royal Court: The Break of Day (and Out of Joint); Pale Horse, Ashes and Sand, The Steward of Christendom (and Out of Joint, Dublin, Sydney), The Editing Process, Peaches, Babies, The Kitchen, Search and Destroy, Women Laughing, Talking in Tongues, Faith Healer.
Other theatre lighting designs include: Three Sisters (Out of Joint, international tour); Disappeared (Leicester Haymarket & tour); Road (Out of Joint tour); The Lodger (Royal Exchange & Hampstead); Richard II, Street Captives (Royal Exchange); Stiff Stuff (Library Theatre, Manchester);Salvation, The Snow Orchid (London Gay Theatre); The Set-Up, Crackwalker (Gate Theatre); Josephine (BAC); Beautiful Thing (Bush, Donmar, Duke of Yorks); over 20 designs for Liverpool Playhouse including Macbeth, The Beaux Stratagem, Madame Mao.
Opera includes: Otello (Opera du Nice);La Traviata, The Magic Flute, The Poisoned Chalice (M.T.L. Donmar, Hamburg, Holland); The Marriage of Figaro, Eugene Onegin, The Abduction from the Seraglio, (Opera 80); The Human Voice, Perfect Swine (MTM).
Currently Chief Electrician at the Royal Court.

The Opportunity of a Lifetime

On September 22, 1995 the Arts Council of England announced that the Royal Court Theatre was to be the recipient of a £16 million Lottery Fund Award. This award has provided the Court with a **once-in-a-lifetime** opportunity to bring this beautiful and important theatre up to date.

The refurbishment will touch all parts of the building, improving facilities for audiences and performers alike. The architects have prepared plans which retain the charm of the historic interior and facade of the Theatre, and the final result is a scheme which will *drastically improve* one of Britain's foremost producing theatres.

However the rules are clear; the Lottery Fund will pay up to three quarters of the costs of our £21 million capital project but the Royal Court must find the remainder itself as Partnership Funding.

This is a challenge we have readily accepted and we are talking with businesses, trust funds and private individuals throughout the country and internationally. Most recently the **New Yorker Magazine** and the **Conde Nast Foundation (USA)** have expressed a commitment to our fund-raising appeal.

In addition, David Suchet has spearheaded a drive which has raised substantial funds from our Friends and audience members. A **tremendous thank-you** to everyone who has generously supported this appeal through single gifts, gift aid and covenanted donations.

> *The name of the Royal Court Theatre is synonymous with freshness, dynamism and vibrancy and its world-wide reputation, for identifying and nurturing talent, is uncontested. As the millennium approaches and our visions of the future take shape, the Theatre is confident that its challenge to raise £5 million towards refurbishing its 100-year old home will be met by vigour, inspiration and conviction.*

For information on how you can play a part in securing our future please call **Jacqueline Simons**, Development Manager, on 0171-823-4132, while for a tour of the theatre before the redevelopment call **Josephine Campbell** on 0171-730-5174.

Invest in the Future

ROYAL COURT THEATRE

share more fully in the life of
the Royal Court Theatre...
become a Patron or Benefactor

Join our supporters, and share in the opportunity
to ensure the continuation of one of the world's
most famous theatres, whilst enjoying a number
of exclusive benefits which will enhance your
theatregoing throughout the year.

For more information please call the
Royal Court Development Office on
0171 823-4132.

THE ROYAL COURT THEATRE

Harry and Me

First published in 1996
by Faber and Faber Limited
3 Queen Square London WC1N 3AU
in association with the Royal Court Theatre
Sloane Square, London SW1N 8AS

Printed in England by Clays Ltd, St Ives plc

Nigel Williams is hereby identified as author of this
work in accordance with Section 77 of the Copyright,
Designs and Patents Act 1988

All rights in this play are strictly reserved and application for performance
etc,. should be made to the author's agent: Judy Daish Associates, 2 St
Charles Place, London, W10 6EG. No performance may be given unless a
licence has been obtained.

A CIP record for this book
is available from the British Library

ISBN 0-571-17819-7

2 4 6 8 10 9 7 5 3 1

Characters

Ray Goodenough
Tracy Maclellan
Harry Harrod

Act One

The programme offices in a television company. A large,
rather shabby room which has housed rather more people
than are in it at present. A lot of empty desks, some
noticeboards with faded messages on and a very great
many telephones. There are very few signs of the pro-
gramme's identity. Perhaps the most potent signal it gives
off is the small, energetic man coming into the room as
the lights go up. He is an almost violently active Jewish
man in middle age – not too smartly dressed – there is a
compelling quality about the passion with which he does
everything. **Ray Goodenough** *– for such is his name –*
rounds the door of the office in a way that calls for, or
rather demands, attention. He is, as he nearly always is,
on the telephone and he acts with this machine the way
some people might dance or make love. His calls are
meant to be enjoyed by the immediate spectator as well as
the invisible recipient. It is about three-thirty on a winter's
afternoon.

Ray Call me, call me, call me, call me. Where am I? I'm
on a mobile, what do you think? Where are you if it
comes to that Harry? You're on your mobile but where
on your mobile? Did I hear seagulls … ? You're breaking
up …

> *Some of this at least is being done for the benefit of a*
> *woman who, because she has seen it all before, is very*
> *wisely ignoring it. She too, as it happens, is on the*
> *phone but is much less interested in performing than*
> *her boss. This is* **Tracy Maclellan**, *a long-serving worker*
> *on the programme for which Ray also works.*

Tracy Well, on the show Harry chats to a celebrity, an ordinary person, and one halfway in between, if you see what I mean. It's sort of Elton John, and a roadsweeper and ... er ... Martin Amis if you get my drift ...

Ray I'm on a mobile phone. On a mobile phone *in the office*. Yes of course there are phones here. There are hundreds of phones here. Terrestrial phones. Earthbound phones. Yes. But I am not *on* a terrestrial phone. I am on a mobile phone Harry *in* the office ... move to a different location ...

Tracy For instance last week we had a woman who had murdered her sister and she was *very* interesting. She had been in prison for eight years and she was *fascinating* about prison life and about, you know, killing her sister which she did with a meat cleaver ...

Ray I'll move ... I'll move ...

Tracy Well a friend of yours has written to us about you, and you are obviously in our Ordinary Person category but I am not sure quite what your story is ...

Ray Because Harry I was *on* the mobile when I walked into the office. I was on the mobile when I was in the foyer, I was on the mobile when I was in the lift, I was on the mobile when I stepped *out* of the lift and into the corridor and I was on the mobile when I rounded the doorway and saw my team doing fuck all with their lives ... Look at them, look at them, look at them, they are completely and utterly hopeless ...

Tracy Them? (*Her phone call is clearly going on and on. She holds her hand over the mouthpiece as she says this.*)

Ray Did you hear me Harry, I said 'them', did you hear me? Remember when it used to be 'them', remember Harry, great days Harry, great days do you remember ...

you recall … (*to Tracy*) He recalls … (*to the phone*) They were all on phones Harry, remember, all working to make the show a great show, they are working their butts off remember? My God they were great days. Tracy – why do I keep talking on the mobile? *Why?*

Tracy Did you say you have boils, is that what you said? (*Her caller clearly starts banging on again. Tracy holds the phone away from her ear.*)

Ray I will tell you why Harry, it is a badge of status! … sure … you have got to show the staff that you can walk and talk at the same time, it is a *badge of status* Harry and that is why I do it, to show I am a free spirit …

Tracy Well the roadsweeper would have to be an ordinary roadsweeper and not a roadsweeper who had written a novel if you see what I mean …

Ray … who knows what I may do next, where I may go next, I may go to the toilet Harry I may … I may go to the toilet …

Tracy … well I suppose they could have done but it would help if it had been a flop …

Ray I'll let you into a secret Harry, *I am in the toilet* … I am talking to you *from the toilet* …

Tracy But we had a deaf and dumb lady one week and one week a woman whose daughter had cerebral palsy …

Ray … because it is the only place I can get any peace and quiet Harry …

Tracy … no, no we didn't have the daughter on, partly because you couldn't understand a word she said but we …

Ray … look where *are* you Harry, I worry when I don't know where you are, I worry about you, I need to be in contact Harry … why do I need to … Harry I am ringing

3

because, in case you didn't remember, we have a studio booked about eighteen hours from now and I am worrying about Dave Hewitt Harry ...

Tracy   ... what I really need to know is a bit more about you unless you are in the celebrity category although, as I say Mr Green, I am afraid I have never heard of you ...

Ray Harry, we have no paperwork Harry, Harry in case you didn't remember you booked this one yourself on account you are such a *big shot* you know his agent like he was your brother and ... Harry I need a number for him, I appreciate he is a *big star* and does not give out his number to know-nothings such as I but I need to book cars, I need to ... Harry I am worried because he is a *big star* and we are on the air as live *tomorrow morning* ... Harry ... (*He stops suddenly. Ray is a highly theatrical character and this should be a highly theatrical moment.*) What do you mean Dave is not coming on the show ... what do you ... *what do you mean by saying that our star celebrity David Hewitt is not coming on the show* ... ? I cannot be hearing you right my friend I ... I cannot be hearing you right ...

Tracy watches open mouthed. Call forgotten. Ray acts up to her interest. Aware that his call is the focus of attention he gives it all he has got.

Harry, Dave Hewitt gave us his word, he gave us his *word* Harry he ... OK he gave you his word. I take it we are in this together Harry, or have I got this wrong ... are we working for *completely separate organizations* ... Harry, tell me this Harry, tell me this, you're the graduate Harry, you have the degree, is he in breach? Is he in breach? Can we sue? Is he in breach?

Tracy oblivious to her call.

Harry how can I find a replacement for Dave Hewitt in ...

4

in no time *at all* … Harry he is a *big star*, Harry you are a friend of his agent, you know this, for Christ's sake Harry he *must* come, you must ring him or his agent and you must say '*he must come on the Harry Harrod Show!*' You must do this. Why? Why has he decided out of the goodness of his heart not to appear … (*As he receives the answer Ray really plays to his waiting drone. A lot of arm waving and eye rolling. Then* …) He saw the show. (*to Tracy*) 'He saw the show.' (*to Harry on the phone*) Who showed him the show for Christ's sake? No one likes the show. I don't like the show. It's disgusting. You know how disgusting it is. It was your idea for Christ's sake. Was it your idea? Or was it mine? I forget. I'm generous. I forget. 'He saw the show.' What are you trying to do to me? I cannot, I cannot, I cannot. I repeat I *cannot* find someone of the calibre of Dave Hewitt by eleven o'clock tomorrow morning …

> *He becomes aware that Tracy is watching him and breaks off from his call to round on his team with insane rage.*

Why are you watching me make a phone call? Is this a new spectator sport? Aren't you on a call Miss Maclellan? Isn't there work to be done? Do I have to do everything on the *Harry Harrod Show* myself, is that it? Is it a *punishment* for being called the producer? Should I have just called myself the *head waiter* or the *bell captain* or something?

Tracy Are you still there Mr Green … ? No, no I was listening, I found it fascinating, we will be in touch … We will let you know Mr Green your … er …

Ray … I was talking to the team Harry, to the team, not to you …

Tracy … skin affliction does sound a fascinating one … we will let you know …

She puts down her phone, lights up and crosses to Ray. She peers over his shoulder as he talks into his mobile. He does not seem to mind this. He talks on …

Ray   … Look what I am saying is – he cannot do this to me. He's doing it to me, to you, to all of us and he cannot be allowed to do it Harry … I have a recording at eleven and it is now nearly four o'clock Harry, at least it is four o'clock in London, England, I don't know, maybe you are phoning me from Venezuela. Harry where are you, I swear I heard seagulls, Harry listen to me … I … *I cannot find anyone of the stature of Dave Hewitt by tomorrow* … Harry do you suggest I just pick up the phone to Paul McCartney or Elton John and say 'Hey guys … doing anything *demain* or would you like to mosey on down to the *Harrod Show*?' … I am not being offensive, I am not, but *I cannot find anyone of the stature of Dave Hewitt by tomorrow* … OK? (*Ray looks across at Tracy.*) I think you should do something Harry … you got us into this, I think you should do something … I cannot find anyone of the stature of Dave Hewitt by tomorrow … (*He holds out the phone. Addresses the office in general.*) He hung up. I said it three times and he hung up. Does that mean he finally got the message? He only really understands when he's been told something three times. (*He speaks to the dead phone.*) You're an asshole. You're an asshole. You're an asshole.

Tracy That's telling him.

Ray What do you want Maclellan? You want money?

Tracy I want to talk to you.

Ray You can't talk to me. I'm busy.

Tracy I don't see why I couldn't have done it. I don't see why I couldn't have booked this …

Ray Hewitt …

Tracy Or whatever he's called. Have I been here too long? Is that it? Are the old guard no longer necessary?

Ray Is that all you want to say to me? 'Are the old guard no longer necessary?' Are we talking Russia 1917 here? Is this it?

Tracy It's about the rumours I've been hearing. I've been hearing rumours about the show and …

Ray About what? Rumours about what?

Tracy About Harry. Rumours that were not good. I want to know if there is any truth in them.

Ray stops. Looks at her.

Ray There is never any truth in rumours. Work Maclellan. Work. I am working. I am about to go to the toilet but *even in the toilet I will be working.* Work work work. Dial dial dial.

Tracy Who do I dial?

Ray Who do you think? Hewitt's agent. Who do you think?

Tracy And who is his agent? May I be allowed to know this? Did our leader vouchsafe this vital piece of information to us?

Ray's gone, brandishing his phone. With great weariness Tracy starts to dial. Almost immediately her other phone goes. She picks it up. As she does so she gets through on the other line.

Tracy Hullo Artists' Bookings? (*very, almost suspiciously, friendly*) Hello, it's Tracy Maclellan here on the *Harry Harrod Show* … yes … the *Harry Harrod Show* … H-A-R-R-O-D yes like the shop … the chat show from hell, sure … Who's this? Derek? Well Derek, do you by any chance happen to know the name of the agent for Dave Hewitt … he's a singer I think … (*She picks up the other line.*) Could you hold please … you … Ray is that you? Where are you? In the … What do you … (*He is obviously giving her an ear bashing.*) I am on the other line. I cannot dial because I am talking to you Ray … I don't want to know that you are in the cubicle Ray … (*She rolls her eyes in despair.*) I am trying to find Dave Hewitt's number Ray … (*to her other call*) Yes … *Dave Hewitt* … yes … he's a musician … no … well … I hadn't heard of him either but … sure I'll hang on thanks … yes, yes I will … Derek … (*She goes to Ray's phone.*) How are you doing Ray? Have you finished? Will you remember to wash your hands? You have gone quiet Ray? Are you totally and utterly absorbed in what you are doing? (*She makes a face to herself. Meanwhile on the other line she has got the number she wants.*) 543 9876 thanks … Thanks Derek, thanks a lot … I'm too old for you Derek and it sounds like you need someone … not necessarily female Derek … thank you Derek … (*She starts to dial another phone. To Ray. Derek from Artists' Bookings has started on to her. She stays with Ray.*) I am now dialling the Peter James Agency OK? They are *Dave Hewitt's agents* OK? I will keep *this* phone close to yours so as you can give me marks for elocution, telephone etiquette and sentence construction OK? (*She is through to the agency.*) Hullo? Is that the Peter James Agency? (*And switches back immediately to Ray.*) Did I hear something flush? You are washing your *hands* that's *good!* Are you enjoying my calls? Do listen, listen, listen! (*to the agency*) Of course I'll hold, that is no problem at all … (*She starts to dial another number. And speaks to Ray as she dials.*) How was that? And now I am making (*as to a child*) another call … (*She is now on three phones and through on the third one.*) Mum … ? Mum … ? This is Tracy … I am

8

still in the office ... no, no, no, I am fine, I am just sick to death of sitting in the same office as that lecherous little bastard Ray Goodenough ... (*to her other phone*) Did you get that? You didn't? I said I was sick to death of sitting in the same office as that lecherous little bastard Ray Goodenough ...

Ray enters, still on the phone. He talks into the phone.

Ray Lecherous little Jewish bastard ...

Tracy Why can't you talk to a person? Why do you always have to use the phone?

Ray And why are you dialling your mother? I thought you were dialling *Dave Hewitt's agent*!

Tracy I'm holding on for them. But I need to call my mother.

Ray is suddenly paranoid.

Ray What's going on? Is something going on that you're not telling me about? Are there changes in your life? Has someone offered you a job?

He now has her attention which is what he wants even though she is on three phones – one of them being to him which is still not disconnected.

Can I ask why, whenever I come into this office, everyone puts down their work and stares at me like they were goldfish? What am I? Am I the Emperor Caligula?

Tracy He is exactly the sort of man we need around here.

Ray And if it is your mother why are you keeping her waiting?

Tracy Because I am talking to you Ray.

Ray (*screeches at her*) And what about Dave Hewitt's

agent? What about the man who represents the man who has had the *nerve* to suggest he is too good for the *Harry Harrod Show*?

Tracy I am waiting. I am waiting on Dave Hewitt's agent.

Ray has started to dial.

Ray If you're on a call, talk. If you're not on a call, make one. Look at me. I am dialling. See? I am dialling!

Indeed he is bashing his mobile furiously. Having only just disconnected it.

Tracy Who are you calling, O Fiddler on the Roof?

Ray I forget. I forget. Who am I calling? All I know is – it's urgent.

Tracy Are you calling Dave Hewitt's agent?

Ray Why should I? Aren't you calling him? Why don't I know who I'm calling? (*rounds on her*) Why don't you know who I am calling? What do I pay you for? Why are you gawping at me? Who are you calling on the other line?

Tracy You.

Ray Haven't you disconnected yet?

Tracy I haven't had time.

Ray And who are you calling on the other line?

Tracy I told you. My mother.

Ray Why are you calling your mother?

Tracy Because I need to speak to her.

Ray Of course! Of course! Stupid of me!

Tracy talks into one of her phones. The one to her mother.

Tracy Yes I was listening Mother ... I'll ask him ... of course ... of course I'll ask him ... (*to Ray*) She says are you still as rude as you ever were?

Ray Tell her I am.

Tracy Did you get that Mother?

Ray is holding up his mobile before pressing SEND.

Ray Who am I calling? It's a mobile number. It must be Harry's mobile. It's engaged. I must be calling Harry. You're calling Hewitt's agent. And your mother. I'm calling Harry. Fine. (*He addresses the office.*) I am being re-routed to his answering machine. Isn't that great?

Tracy doesn't answer. She lights another cigarette.

Ray Work! Make phone calls! We have a crisis! Call agents! Get in touch with celebrities! Work Maclellan! Work! Work! Work!

Tracy Mother I want you to do something for me – the second post should be in, could you go and see if there's a letter for me ... an ... official-looking letter OK? (*Her mother starts to bang on at her and we should see that Tracy is talking to a voluble, if not senile, old lady.*) I know it's a long way downstairs Mother but ... no it will not wait Mother it ... thank you ... thank you ...

Ray is listening to this conversation with much interest. Tracy rounds on him.

Work. Make phone calls! Work! (*back to her mother*) And if it's there Mother could you open it and read it to me ... yeah ... yeah thanks ... yeah I'll wait ... I know it's a long way down but ... thanks ... thanks ... thank you ... (*She hears activity on her other phone. Picks it up.*) Yes I am holding for Peter James, I want to speak to him about David Hewitt, this is Tracy Maclellan from the

Harry Harrod Show thank you, yes I see … well I'll wait.

The answer machine message has ended. Ray talks into the phone.

Ray Harry this is Ray, I need to talk to you about Hewitt. I have a call into the agent but I need to know what you think Harry. Maybe you should talk to the agent because you know him. You could sweet-talk him. In which case we shouldn't talk to him first. Maybe that's it. Maybe you should call the agent and we shouldn't. Thanks for your help on this Harry. (*He presses* END *and looks at Tracy as if this was the first time he was aware of her or that she was doing anything of importance.*) Who are you calling?

Tracy Dave Hewitt's agent. You told me to.

Ray Did I?

Tracy Of course you did.

Ray You mustn't jump the gun Maclellan. You mustn't let me make wrong decisions.

Tracy How do I do that?

Ray Don't call Dave Hewitt's agent. Whatever else you do don't call him.

Tracy Why not?

Ray I talked it through with Harry's machine. Don't whatever you do call Dave Hewitt's agent.

Tracy I have a call into him.

Ray Not before we've thought what to say. We have to be very, very careful and diplomatic here. He is a big powerful agent and we don't want to offend his client even though his client is a complete cunt and we hate him.

Tracy is about to disconnect her phone when someone comes on at the agency end.

Tracy Hullo ... yes ... this is Tracy Maclellan from the *Harry Harrod Show* you are ... Mrs Parker right and you ... take your other call Mrs Parker, of course I'll wait, Mrs Parker ...

Ray is doing a lot of oh-what-a-tragedy acting. Tracy shrugs. What can she do now she is waiting on them?

Tracy What do we say?

Ray That's what I am saying, what do we say? (*He paces.*) Get me Harry on the mobile while I think what we say. Maybe I should talk to Harry before I talk to Dave Hewitt's agent. He has two mobiles. He has two mobiles. Call his other mobile. Maybe he has both mobiles with him. Listen why not? Isn't he in the communication business? You have to call Harry. Call Harry. Maybe Harry should call Dave Hewitt personally. He knows Dave Hewitt. I think he does. *Maybe I should call Harry before I call Dave Hewitt or his agent!*

Tracy Maybe we should call them all at the same time and hold the phones together.

Ray Fuck off Maclellan.

Tracy I am holding on for his assistant, can I just disappear? Isn't that rude?

Ray It's rude. *Don't do it!*

Tracy When they put me through what do I say?

Ray You say ... (*He paces.*) 'I am on my knees before you, I am begging you, I am licking your arse, I am prostrating myself before you and offering you my tired old buttocks, I am eating humble pie, I am eating shit, I am worshipping you and your agency, I am beseeching you

13

and imploring you and I am saying that if you allow your client to appear on the *Harry Harrod Show* with a three-hundred-year-old tetraplegic from Taunton I will personally take your foreskin between my two front teeth and squeeze it backwards and forwards and forwards and backwards over the glans penis until semen rises like a mountain stream deep in your foaming prostate and surges like an avalanche up the vas deferens and in the direction of my eager-to-please mouth.'

Tracy I don't think I can say that.

Ray OK don't say it.

Tracy What shall I say? (*Tracy has, as instructed, been dialling Harry, and has finally got a ringing tone.*) We are on line to the boss.

Ray To who?

Tracy To Harry. I got you Harry. I got you your presenter and executive producer.

Ray What are you saying?

Tracy Ray it is ringing, Ray you are on line to Harry –

Ray Harry?

Tracy Harry Harrod. This is the *Harry Harrod Show*.

Ray Hi!

Tracy Ray it is Harry. I have got through to his second mobile. And it is ringing. He may be searching his pockets for it even as we speak.

Ray is not listening to her at all.

Ray Maybe we should just scream at Hewitt's agent you know? Maybe we should say – (*screams*) 'Fuck off, fuck off, fuck off, you dumb, dumb cunt, I don't care if my

14

show is watched by only one quadraplegic person's friends, I don't fucking care, fuck you, fuck you, fuck you, fuck you very much, fuck, fuck, fuck you and good fucking night!'

He is close enough to both Tracy's phones for this outburst to be clearly audible to both Harry and whoever is at the end of the agency line. And in fact Tracy registers that the invisible Mrs Parker has registered something.

Tracy Mrs Parker hi … no, no, no, that was just … er someone in the … er … next-door office … of course I don't mind holding Mrs Parker … (*She covers the mouthpiece.*) I think she got most of that Ray.

Ray How did she seem? Did she seem impressed?

Tracy I think she liked it Ray.

Ray We were really screaming …

Tracy We? We?

Ray Who is she, this Mrs Parker? What's in this for her? Why is she making you wait? Is she listening in to our conversation? Is she taping us do you think? Are Hewitt's lawyers listening in at that end, listening to us and the way we carry on?

Tracy Us? We?

There are now four phones in front of Tracy. She has two to her ear – the calls to Harry's mobile and to Hewitt's agent and another two on the desk in front her, one of which is the call to her mother and the other the disconnected call from Ray's mobile. Ray picks up the abandoned receiver on the desk. And talks into it cautiously.

Ray Mrs Parker? Are you still there? (*no answer*) Hullo?

Mrs Parker? (*to Tracy*) She's gone very quiet.

Tracy That's because she has to go down the stairs, out into the hall and climb back up and she is eighty-four and has a hip replacement.

Ray How come you know so much about Dave Hewitt's agent's assistant?

Tracy That isn't Dave Hewitt's agent's assistant.

Ray Who the fuck is it?

Tracy It's my mother.

Ray (*goes barmy*) What the fuck do you think you are doing? Do you think that because we work in a leisure industry we are all supposed to sit around doing nothing? Why are you phoning your mother?

Tracy I *told you* Ray. Or rather you *made sure you overheard*. I want her to read me a letter.

Ray That's right. You're right. You're expecting a letter. You've got another job. You hate me. You think I'm a bastard. Why are you doing this to me? Why are you treating me the way *Dave Hewitt* treats me? How can you and he behave like this to me Maclellan? How have you the nerve to carry on as if *this is the worst show ever in the whole history of television*. For Christ's sake.

Tracy Because it is.

Ray *Only we are allowed to say that.* Because we are family. This is a crisis Maclellan, I need to talk to Harry. I need a conversation with him. Where is he?

Tracy I don't know where he is. He may be in the Natural History Museum. He may be in an Italian restaurant. He may be in the third row of the stalls of the Royal National Theatre groping around in his briefcase while some poor thespians try to make the last act of John Gabriel Borkmann audible above the bleat of his mobile phone. All I *know* is that I am through to his second mobile and that his second mobile is ringing.

Tracy hands Harry the other phone by her ear. He takes the receiver and starts to pace about the office again. As he does so Mrs Parker comes on the line to Tracy.

Tracy Mrs Parker hi … it's about Dave Hewitt … your client Dave Hewitt … I know … the thing is he is planning to come on our show tomorrow … the *Harry Harrod Show*, I think Harry … I sent you a letter confirming the contract if you want to check the file, I am sure that … we try to be organized Mrs Parker … yes do look for it … if you want me to hold I will hold, it is no trouble …

Ray Harry where are you? (*He listens.*) He's in a bar.

Tracy Oh my God. Get him out of there.

Ray Harry, get out of there Harry.

Tracy Ask him what he's drinking.

Ray Harry what are you drinking? (*He listens.*) Tomato juice. He's drinking tomato juice.

Tracy Now ask him what he's drinking with it.

Ray Harry what are you drinking with it? (*He listens.*) Triple vodka.

Tracy Get him out of there.

Ray Get out of there Harry. (*He listens.*) And a beer on the side.

Tracy Tell him he must leave. Now.

Ray You must leave. Now. (*He listens.*) And an

17

Armagnac. For later. (*to the phone*) ... Harry, is it that no one wants to be on the show, Harry is that what is depressing you and bringing you down, is that it? Harry we mustn't think like that, Harry we have ... we have ... Harry we have *Dave Hewitt* for Christ's sake ... no I know we don't have him but we have to think positive about this, he said ... Harry *before he went off the idea he was very positive about it* ... Harry, Dave Hewitt is a *big star* ... Harry he has had number one hits Harry ... (*to Tracy*) He says where.

Tracy Where what?

Ray Where has Dave Hewitt had number one hits?

Tracy shrugs.

Don't just sit there shrugging Maclellan get on to it. Get the research department on to it.

Tracy has lifted the phone from the desk. The one to her mother.

Tracy Mother hi, back yet ... ? No ... ? Mother?

Ray is talking to Harry.

Ray Bear with me Harry, we are looking into this. We are on to this Harry. (*Covers mouthpiece. Screeches at Tracy.*) Find out where Hewitt had these hits and get the information to me prontissimo. My God, who do I have to fuck to get anything done around here? Make calls. Dial. Dial. Dial.

Tracy Who do you suggest I dial?

Ray The people who know about these things. Ask his agent's assistant for Christ's sake. If she ever condescends to answer that phone you are clutching to your earhole. If the conceited lazy bitch Mrs Parker, or whatever she chooses to call herself instead of Whore-With-Ever-

Dripping-Fanny or whatever her *real name* happens to be should deign to come down off her perch and speak to the scumbags of the *Harry Harrod Show*!

He has got close enough to Tracy for this speech to be clearly heard at the other end of her call.

Tracy Mrs Parker hi, did you get all that?

Ray expresses horror. Tracy smiles sweetly.

She is looking for a letter that has no chance whatsoever of being there …

Ray What letter?

Tracy The letter I have written confirming Mr Dave Hewitt's contract.

Ray Why isn't it there?

Tracy Because I didn't write it.

Ray You didn't write it? My God! You didn't write it? My God! Maclellan! How long have you worked here? Why didn't you write it?

Tracy Because we have no contract with Dave Hewitt.

Ray Why have we no contract with Dave Hewitt?

Tracy Because you said Harry was his agent's friend. And it would be OK.

Ray I said that?

Tracy You did Ray.

Ray Are you going to tell her that? Are you going to tell this Mrs Parker … this agent's assistant, that we have no contract with her client for him to break?

Tracy What do you think?

Ray I don't know what to think.

Tracy I can hardly let her know that we have absolutely no position on the person we have hired through her can I?

Ray You can't. You are in her hands. (*He stops, as realization dawns.*) We are in her hands. (*sudden, violent anger*) How come the stupid bitch has the nerve to treat us like this? Why does this stuck-up lesbian cow not unstrap her fucking dildo and take her index finger out of her secretary's anus and talk to us? Are we all diseased on the *Harry Harrod Show* for fuck's sake? Who does this bitch think she is?

Tracy Mrs Parker hi, you're back with us ... no, no, no, just the next-door office again ... it's a board meeting ... that's all ... it isn't filed under the *Harry Harrod Show* ... ? Well maybe you filed it under our producer's name ... Ray Goodenough ...

Ray is talking to Harry.

Ray Harry you mustn't be so negative and you must get out of there. You know you shouldn't drink Harry. Why? Why shouldn't you drink? (*Rolls his eyes at Tracy.*) Because you are an alcoholic, Harry. Remember? Remember why you joined that club where you sit around with all the other friends of Dorothy or whatever they are called and talk about your problems. You must get out of there Harry. (*He screeches to Tracy.*) I need this information on Hewitt. I need to calm him down Maclellan. He is in bad shape out there.

Back to Harry. Tracy has started to dial furiously.

Harry. Harry? Hullo? Who am I speaking to?

Tracy Hullo, I wonder if you could help me Library this is Tracy Maclellan from the *Harry Harrod Show* and I am trying to find some facts out about a musician called Dave Hewitt ...

Ray Would you please put my friend back on the line please?

Tracy No he's alive ... I wanted to know where he has had chart hits ...

Ray ... And would you give him back his phone please? (*He is getting an ear bashing.*) That is not your mobile phone. I do not care how much he has had to drink you have no right to take away his phone. And you have no right to talk to me like that I am warning you ... (*more ear bashing*)

Tracy Finland? You think. Not Finland. Norway you think. Maybe. Not Norway. Sweden perhaps. Not Sweden. He must have had a hit somewhere. Taiwan? (*She is now on two lines again and the call to her mother is still on her desk. She lifts it up and listens while on her other calls but the old lady is obviously not yet back.*) Mrs Parker hi, yes Tracy Maclellan still here ... You don't have a file under Goodenough?

Ray Fuck off. Fuck off. Fuck off.

Tracy ... well I'm surprised ...

Ray Up your fucking arse. (*He is at screaming pitch.*)

Tracy Perhaps it's under my name ...

Ray Come over here and fucking say that ...

Tracy ... that's Tracy Maclellan ...

Ray Fuck you up your arse cuntface ...

Tracy Yes the board do get a little heated sometimes. I think they are discussing bad language on television ... no, I'm in no hurry ...

Ray I am warning … I am warning you you *cunt* that if you carry on using my friend's mobile phone I will call the police and send them round to wherever you are, where are you … ? The Ferret and Firkin right, right, right you *cunt* … (*He turns to Tracy.*) Call the police. Send them round to the Ferret and Firkin. Say we want to report the theft of a mobile phone.

Tracy Which Ferret and Firkin?

Ray talks to his mobile.

Which Ferret and Firkin? (*She talks to library.*) Yes, yes, yes, if you can find out *any more* on Dave Hewitt could you fax those cuttings through to us … sure is there really nothing else?

Ray has been listening to his caller from the Ferret and Firkin. Turns to Tracy.

Ray You know the one you cunt. Apparently. (*to phone*) Don't use fucking language like that to me you asshole. (*to Tracy*) The Ferret and Firkin on the dark side of the moon, where little goblins go with sharp, sharp teeth. Apparently.

Tracy Is he drunk?

Ray They're all drunk. (*to phone*) Who am I talking to now? Who are you? What is your name? (*to Tracy*) He's called Kevin You Cunt. I think they are passing it round the fucking bar. (*To phone. A new caller has appeared.*) Oh hi! (*to Tracy*) This one sounds quite reasonable. (*to phone*) Look. Would you do something for me? Would you go over to the man in glasses with silver hair and tell him …

Tracy is on her call to Library.

Tracy Dave Hewitt has not had a hit anywhere in the

world not even in Zambia and he is a total and utter loser.

Ray Dave Hewitt has not had a hit anywhere in the world not even in Zambia and he is a total and utter loser.

Tracy Thanks for all your help.

Ray Thanks for all your help. (*panic*) Don't say that. Don't say that to the man in glasses. Don't please say that to the man in glasses. Keep the phone. Just don't say that to the man in ... (*ear bashing*) Harry? Harry? Just kidding. Just kidding. Harry get out of there. You are getting out of there. They are throwing you out of there. Let them throw you Harry. Let them throw you. Go along with it Harry. It is the best thing you can do Harry.

> *Tracy is back on to Mrs Parker.*

Tracy Mrs Parker, our editor and presenter Mr Harry Harrod, who is quite a distinguished figure in his own way, wrote to you and ... (*getting quite heated*) perhaps it's filed under chat shows ... ? You will ... ? Well in that case I will wait ...

> *Someone else has taken over Harry's mobile. Ray is going crazy.*

Ray Don't you speak to me like that you cunt. Don't you speak to me like that. If my friend is in any way damaged I will ... where are you ... you are not in Albania ha ha ha ha you are ... in Fulham ... right and now you are going to throw the phone after him ... fine ... fine well I am telling you that the police will be ... (*He holds the phone away from him.*) What are they doing there? Tracy. Tracy. Where are we?

> *He holds the phone to her. She is now only on to one call, apart from her mum. She listens.*

Tracy In a blender it sounds like.

Ray Call him on his other mobile. He has another mobile.

Tracy Is it on his person?

Ray We have no way of knowing.

Tracy Is he up to answering it?

Ray I have no way of knowing. But call him. Let him know about Dave Hewitt's agent. (*in sudden fury*) What has happened with Dave Hewitt's agent? Why are you not keeping me up to date on the Dave Hewitt's agent's assistant thing?

Tracy Because you have been too busy.

Ray Too busy doing what?

Tracy Too busy screaming at people in pubs and telling them they are cunts.

Ray What is the situation with this Mrs Parker then?

Tracy We are still hanging on while she checks the correspondence.

> *Ray, in a rage, picks up the phone on the desk and screams into it.*

Ray Listen you stupid old bag, why don't you stop fucking about and do us all a fucking favour and talk to us, say something even if it is only that you are being shagged up the arse by a tame donkey. (*Listens. Hands phone to Tracy.*) It's your mother.

Tracy Hi Mother!

Ray Why are you calling your mother?

Tracy I need to ask her about this letter.

Ray Why do you think *you have the time* to call your

mother?

Tracy Because I am waiting for Dave Hewitt's agent's assistant to get back on the line to me about a letter that I know for certain does not exist. I think I probably have time not only to phone my mother but also to prepare and bring to the table a dish of the meatballs you so enjoy and spaghetti with a tomato salad on the side.

Ray I love meatballs.

Tracy I know. (*to phone*) Mother, sorry, was the letter there? Did the letter arrive?

Ray Meatballs are my favourite.

Tracy Well Mother, sometimes they leave them at the flat door. Could you bear to go down to the basement and look … ? Yes, yes, yes, it is important … yes I … sure I'll hang on sure … I know your leg is … but … thank you … thanks … (*She waits.*) What's with this letter? (*She displays real annoyance with him. Almost for the first time.*) Don't listen in to my private calls. (*She clicks off her phone.*)

Ray You hung up. You hung up on your mother.

Tracy I want to talk to her in private.

Ray Then why did you phone her when I was in the room?

Tracy Why did I phone her when you were in the room?

Ray That's what I am asking.

Tracy It's a good question.

Ray has got action on his mobile.

Ray Hullo … hullo … who is this … ? Who am I talking to … ? Hullo sir … hullo sir … that is very very kind of you sir … sir this phone belongs to a Mr Harry Harrod

who … you have … you saw the show? That's great …
you saw the … I am sorry … I am sorry … sir I am not
interested in your opinion of the show sir …

Mrs Parker has come back on the line.

Tracy Well if you really can't find it let's dispense with
talking about the letter, but the fact of the matter is that
Mr Hewitt did make an undertaking to appear on the
show …

Ray Sir, listen I just want … look I do not like the tone
you are taking with me on this I … oh *fuck off* please …
just *fuck off* and die why don't you, you …

Tracy Perhaps you could give me Hewitt's number …
well all right then, ask Mr James …

Ray *I demand to know if you can see the owner of this
phone anywhere in the vicinity, it is not your phone* …
Harry Harrod is paying for this call, you asshole, he is
paying for you to insult me and him and I do not … (*to
Tracy*) They are all drunk out there. All of them. Call
Harry. On his other mobile.

Tracy If it is on his person …

Ray Call him.

Tracy If you say so, o mine fuehrer. (*She starts to dial.*)

Ray You can't see a thing? Well we will have to help you
along won't we you ignorant bastard … don't you talk to
me like that …

Tracy Hullo Harry? (*to Ray*) I got Harry.

Ray Give him to me. (*He takes the phone from her.*)
What is with Hewitt's agent?

Tracy She won't give out the number. It's top secret
apparently.

Ray Why are we dealing with the assistant and not the boss? (*to Tracy's phone*) Harry are you OK ... ? You are ... you are sitting down, that's good Harry ... Harry listen to me carefully ... *can you see anyone else near by?* (*to his mobile*) Yeah well fuck off you cunt, fuck, fuck off and up your arse you cunt and right up it with a bargepole, you carry on talking, the vengeance of God will strike you I swear it, the hand of God will find you out ... (*to Tracy's phone*) There's a guy on the other side of the street with a mobile phone ... Harry that is *your* mobile phone ... *stay where you are Harry* ... how big is he Harry ... ? Small, really small with glasses ... that's good Harry, that is good, and he is facing away from you, that is better Harry ... now move close up to him Harry ...

Tracy (*to phone, starting to get ratty*) He won't let us have the number? Why not?

Ray Now Harry, you will only get one crack at this Harry ... when I say go I want you to bring the mobile down on his head as hard as you can OK? And then I want you to push the bastard in the small of the back and grab the phone off him and run like hell. Have you got that ... ? Good, good ... (*to stolen mobile*) Fuck off, fuck off, fuck off, I tell you you are going to be punished for using foul language to me in that way ...

    Tracy is getting her ear bashed.

Tracy Oh no you do not Mrs Parker, you hear no such thing, this office is full of dedicated professional people who do not say ...

Ray Cunt!

Tracy Very often.

    Ray pauses. Then to Harry's phone.

Ray Go!

Tracy How's he doing?

Ray It's breaking up.

Tracy is back in with Mrs Parker.

Tracy I am accusing *you* of unprofessional behaviour Mrs Parker and I am saying … please do not use that kind of language with me …

Ray (*to Harry's phone*) Harry can you hear me, Harry are you there, come in Harry, come in Harry … (*He is getting no answer. He listens to the stolen mobile.*) How does that feel you bastard? (*hearing something*) Harry it's you! You're back! Harry get out of there Harry! Run Harry! Run! (*to Tracy*) I'm getting him in stereo. (*to both phones*) Run Harry. This is great. Run Harry. Run with the ball.

Tracy I must protest Mrs Parker, in the strongest possible terms, Mrs Parker I do not feel that …

Ray becomes aware of her. Winces.

Ray (*to Tracy*) You're talking to Dave Hewitt's agent?

Tracy His assistant. Isn't that what I was supposed to do?

Ray Why are you talking to Dave Hewitt's agent's assistant like that? Why are you being confrontational Maclellan?

Tracy I must have learned it from someone. (*to her phone*) … the *Harry Harrod Show* is not quote 'a pile of shit' unquote … it …

Ray almost runs across the office.

Ray What did she say?

Tracy Nothing Ray.

Ray What did she say? (*He is now by her side. Listening* *in to the call.*) Give me the phone.

Tracy Ray – be tactful …

Ray What do you take me for Maclellan?

Tracy Don't be confrontational.

Ray Who do you think I am Maclellan? Do you think that landing this *big fish* Hewitt is not important to me? Do you think I don't care about Harry's morale? Give me the phone. (*to Harry, on the two phones*) Keep going Harry, keep running, I have you in stereo Harry, keep on going!

Tracy holds up the phone for him as he has no hands free.

Tracy Be charming. Even if she insults the *Harry Harrod Show* OK?

Ray She insulted the show?

Tracy And be *calm.* (*She holds up the phone.*)

Ray I won't listen Maclellan. I'll be calm. I won't listen. I'll wait for her to stop then I'll be calm. (*to Harry's phones*) You're doing great Harry! Keep on running Harry! (*He mutters to himself.*) Fuck off you bastard, I hate you, I hate you, you cunt, fuck right off up your ass, you asshole. (*breathes deeply*) Work it out of the system. (*And at last he speaks to the irate Mrs Parker. He is very, very sweet and charming.*) Mrs Parker hi! … Can I speak to Pete? This is Ray Goodenough from the *Harry Harrod Show* … the chat show … yes the chat show from hell, sure it –

Tracy Ray –

Ray Is, sure it is, ha, ha, ha, ha, it's a disaster but we have to work to make a living. Can I talk with Pete please, is that possible … ? He's busy … sure, sure, sure I'll wait … you think he might be some time, that is fine, I'll wait as long as you like … (*to the Harry phones*) Stay away from the policemen Harry. Keep on the other side of the street from the policemen Harry … (*to Mrs Parker*) Well Mrs Parker I don't *mind* talking with you, of course I do not, but my researcher didn't seem to be getting anywhere and I am a personal friend of Pete's … (*to Harry phones, shouting*) Run faster you stupid bastard! (*to Mrs Parker*) No, no, no Mrs Parker just … office aerobics, you know, I think if I talked to Pete … you don't think he wants to speak to me …

Tracy Ray –

Ray Whatever gave you the idea that he didn't want to speak to me? Have I done something wrong? And if I have may I know what it is so as I can, you know, *apologize* … ?

Tracy Ray –

Ray He told you he didn't want to speak to me. Well, well, well, that is pretty direct and straightforward. I hate being lied to and that is very honest of you and I appreciate your honesty –

Tracy Ray –

Ray I hate being lied to and although you are being honest and straightforward about this whole thing of not wanting to talk to me, as if I had, you know, *a communicable disease*, ha, ha, ha, it is probably true to say, is it not, that Pete or Dave or both of them together told a teensy tiny little porky when they said that Dave wanted to be on the *Harry Harrod Show* …

Tracy Ray –

  Ray talks on Harry's phones.

Ray Keep on running Harry! Keep on fucking running man! (*to Mrs Parker, ultra reasonable*) Well if Dave wants to change his mind that is his privilege, we have had some problems with the show I agree, and in terms of taste we don't always hit it, I found the man who had his penis cut off rather moving actually, I thought he spoke well and ... sure ... well he wanted to wave it around in the glass jar that came from him, look ...

Tracy Ray –

Ray I don't really want to listen to you insulting the show because some people enjoy it and still watch and I do not see really why we should listen to people like you who ... well what have you ever done?

Tracy Ray –

Ray What the fuck have you ever done you dumb bitch, what in the name of motherfucking Jesus have you ever done but stick your finger up your twat in the offices of some little cunt who makes a living out of total and utter losers like Dave Hewitt, who has not even had a fucking hit in fucking Finland for Christ's fucking sake ...

Tracy has her head in her hands.

... I don't care if he has an 'Indie reputation' to protect, I don't care if he is an up and coming singer-songwriter, to me he is a total and utter cunt and he lied to me and Harry and the show and you are a fucking cunt, you are. (*He looks at the phone.*) She hung up.

Tracy They do.

Ray They have no stamina. Call her back.

Tracy No.

Ray Call her back.

Tracy No.

Ray I'll deal with you later. (*to his stereo phones*) Harry is that you? Harry are you there? (*to Tracy*) He is going to see his ex-wife.

Tracy Which ex-wife?

Ray Harry which ex-wife? (*to Tracy*) June.

  Tracy flinches.

Tracy Not June. Tell him to stay away from June. She'll kill him. If I were June I'd kill him.

Ray He's going to see her. She lives in Fulham.

Tracy Tell him not to do that.

Ray Don't do that Harry. (*to Tracy*) Is that what brought this on?

Tracy Was he weird when you rang before?

Ray He was like … it was like he wasn't there. You know?

Tracy I know.

Ray Harry – (*to his phones*) I was talking to Tracy. What did you say brought this on? What did you say? (*to Tracy*) His son brought this on. (*shrugs*) I didn't even know he had a son. (*to his phones*) Harry I didn't even know you had a son. (*to Tracy, real surprise and concern*) He hung up.

Tracy Yeah?

Ray And he was crying.

Tracy Yeah?

Ray On both phones. He was crying.

Tracy Yeah?

Ray Why would he cry like that?

Tracy He was talking to *you*. On two phones at the same time.

Ray (*sitting, for the first time in the play*) Why would he do that? Why would he cry? Why would he do that?

Tracy Why would he do that?

Ray Call him.

Tracy On which phone?

Ray On both phones. Use my mobile. Let him know we care.

Tracy Do I dial the numbers at the same time? Or do you want the experience to happen serially?

Ray How long have you worked for me Maclellan?

Tracy Fifteen years four months and thirteen days.

Ray Were you counting?

Tracy Every minute of every day.

Ray That's good. You knew what was happening to you. That's good. You should know what's going down in your life. And why.

Tracy Why did you ask me?

Ray Why did I ask you what?

Tracy Why did you ask me how long I have been working for you?

Ray I wanted to ask you if I had deprived you of all initiative.

Tracy Do you still want to ask me that?

Ray I think I do.

Tracy You have.

Ray I am sorry. I am truly, deeply sorry. (*He puts his head in his hands.*)

Tracy I'll dial both numbers at the same time. The shock might be therapeutic. He'll think he's about to burst into flames.

  Tracy dials. Ray gets up.

Ray What are we doing with our lives Maclellan? Why are we letting them slip away like this? Why haven't we done more with our lives? Why have we been stuck in this office for the last fifteen years?

Tracy I don't know.

Ray Why did I never fuck you Maclellan? Why did I fuck all the others but not you? Was I repulsive to you? Were you repulsive to me? Why didn't it happen?

Tracy We were too important to each other.

Ray Of course. Stupid of me.

Tracy Anyway you did fuck me.

Ray When did I do that?

Tracy If you can't remember I am not telling you.

Ray What was it like?

Tracy It was amazing.

Ray Was it?

Tracy No.

Ray No. (*suddenly weary*) It never is with me.

Tracy Harry … Harry … (*to Ray*) He says hold on, his

other phone is going. (*to Harry*) Harry that is me on the other line. Should you pick it up? If you want me in stereo pick it up. (*to Ray*) He's picking it up.

Ray gestures to her. He wants his mobile. She tosses it to him. He talks into both phones at the same time.

Ray Harry, you are getting me in stereo Harry. And I want to advise you *not to go and see your ex-wife.* Because Harry … Harry … Harry … remember why you left her Harry? Remember what you said about her in Langan's Brasserie the day the divorce came through, Harry … Think back Harry, think back … I am not going to quote your own words to you Harry but what you said to me was … well … it was … harsh … *all I am saying is that June is not who you need to see at this time …*

Tracy Maybe it's to do with his son. Maybe that's why he's going to see her …

Ray They never had a son. Call June.

Tracy I can't do that.

Ray Why can't you do that?

Tracy She knows my voice.

Ray So?

Tracy She knows your voice. Remember?

Ray Remember what?

Tracy How we covered for him. How we covered for the little rat.

Ray When –

Tracy When he was with Sue. Or Prue. Or Lou or whatever she was called.

Ray Sue –

35

Tracy Or maybe it was Sue *and* Prue ...

Ray Don't call her. (*He paces.*) No. You must call her. You have to call her. If she gets hold of Harry we won't have a show tomorrow. And call Dave Hewitt's agent. But don't say who you are to either of them. Whatever you do don't say you are from the *Harry Harrod Show*.

Tracy Why should I do that? People scream at you. Who do I call first?

Ray All of them. (*He winces. Harry is clearly getting emotional at the other end.*)

Tracy Be careful with him.

Ray Harry you said ... you said she was a witch. You said she sucked you dry. You said she had a deformed soul. You said that sex with her was like masturbating into sandpaper. And that was when it was good. (*to Tracy*) He hung up.

Tracy Did he cry?

Ray He sort of gurgled. Call him back.

Tracy I am on two calls already you stupid ignorant Jewish bastard.

As Ray punches out Harry's mobile number he rants.

Ray Why is it that you seem to have acquired, over the years you have worked for me, a kind of *resistance,* a kind of *allergy* to using the very instrument that I pay you to employ? Is it that you have a sort of finite number of telephone calls within you and that you are reaching the end of your dialling life – (*He has got one line ringing.*) He is not answering. I'll call his other number.

Tracy has got through on one line. She affects a Scottish accent.

Tracy Hullo is that the Peter James Agency … my name is
Fiona Macrae from Scottish International Television, I am
the executive producer of a television programme which
… er … you probably will not have heard of … er …
down South … What is it called … ? Well it's called the …
er … *Hamish MacHeggarty Show* and I am interested in
one of your … er … musicians a Mr *Hewitt* aye och aye
Mr David Hewitt … aye I'll bide a wee while …

Ray has got through on the other line.

Ray Harry – this is Ray Harry … I know your other
phone is going that is me Harry, I am making it ring … I
am not the Antichrist Harry … pick it up could you …

*Tracy has got through on her line. She affects an
African accent.*

Tracy Hullo … is dat Mrs Harrod … here is speakin'
Gwenda Amkalume from de Alcoholics Anonymous Club
… I am ringin' because one of de members heah is on his
way to your house and we tink he may be dangerous and
you mus' not let him in Mrs Harrod … it is your husban'
de television personality Mistah Henry Harrod … Missy
Harrod everyone have some personality even Mistah
Henry Harrod is not totally beneath contempt. At de club
we all fin' him most amusin' …

Tracy switches to Scottish as Ray talks into his mobile.

Ray Well find it Harry … it is ringing somewhere on
your person … unless you've swallowed it … look for it
Harry …

Tracy is giving her all.

Tracy … nay nay I'll bide a muckle if ye'll bide a muckle
ye ken … a muckle doesnae fash a ha'pence as we say in
Lochinbagel and in the Glen MacSchnorrer!

Ray Maclellan –

But Tracy is well away. She is in African mode on her other line.

Tracy Hallo dere Missy Harrod … yaaas ah am heah … dis am a big office an' de people ringin' in all de time t'reatenin' to commit de suicide an' so on … Ah am shocked to hear you say dat you t'ink dat in your husban's case dat would be a good idea ah … (*She hears something on her other line. Switches in on the call in Scottish.*) Och it's nae trouble tae wait a wee while an' bide while the glans is forrit … I'll bide frae Mister James the bonny man an' he cannae dash a few canny slubbies wi' hisself he cannae be far frae hoosin' aboot as we say in Drumforboglehoose …

Ray Maclellan –

Tracy Aye tartan tae my trews young lady, I was born in the Firth of Forth and 'weekit ma slime' in the big glen yonder away behind the Old Man of Drunmanmuire …

Ray Maclellan –

Tracy I have my other line going away there ye'll pardon me. (*She picks up the phone to Harry's wife, in Scottish*) Mrs Harrod I ken well – (*switches to African*) Dat you must not allow de husband on to de premises on account of de fact dat he is extremely dangerous … ah would recommend dat you take a shufti out of de window of de house assumin' dat you do have de window ha, ha, ha, my little jokin' an' see if you can see him approachin' …

Ray Maclellan you must stop this … (*to his phone*) You've found the phone Harry, that's good, now answer it Harry, that's good, hullo Harry – now *where are you Harry* … coming up to her block of flats Harry – listen you are not to get down about this Dave Hewitt thing – we are on to his agent now and …

Tracy Hullo is that Mr James – a verra guid mornin' tae ye –

Ray Maclellan –

Tracy I was calling you from the *Hamish MacHeggarty Show* which is a Scottish cultural programme that features serious musicians of the quality and calibre of … say … David Hewitt …

Ray *That's more like it* … try and book him for tomorrow …

> *Tracy is being slightly more restrained than she was. Ray goes back to his Harry phones.*

Harry –

Tracy Tell him to wave his arms above his head.

Ray Why?

Tracy Just do it. (*to Dave Hewitt's agent*) Nae nae Mister James there's nocht here but us chickens ye ken … *who is Hamish MacHeggarty* och he's a verra well-known cultural figure … He has written novels … What novels … ? Well *The Braes are Singing* for example was verra, verra successful –

Ray Maclellan –

> *But Tracy is already on to her other phone. Tracy is African.*

Tracy Missy Harrod I wants to know if you can see a man wavin' de arms above de head in de street outside … (*She indicates to Ray that he should get Harry to do just this.*) Ah am sure dat dat is de kind of t'ing he will be doin' Missy Harrod on account he is de very strange state of mind … dere is a man dere … ?

Ray Harry I want you to wave your arms above your head …

Tracy There was a book of love poetry called *The Loch is Full of Fish*, there was an autobiography called simply *Autobiography* and – could you bide a while? (*She is in trouble on her other line. Putting her hand over the phone to James she does a quick African.*) Dat is a complex question Missy Harrod – I'm not sure if I can answer that … I know – ah will hand you over to our senior man Mr Kwame Obolonga who will enlighten you as to de policy and practice of dis branch of de Alcoholics Anonymous! (*And she thrusts the phone at a horrified Ray.*)

Ray Missy Harrod may I help you, ah am Kwame Obolonga, Senior Man at dis branch of de Alcoholics Anonymous and … yes yes we are all African heah on account we are … mah voice mat be familiar but I do not t'ink we have met Missy Harrod … ah am six foot t'ree and as black as your hat …

Tracy Yes Mr James.

Ray Well … perhaps ah can help you wid de problem of de very dangerous man who is even now approachin' your flat … He is wavin' de arms above de head? Dat is a ver' ver' bad sign Missy Harrod … an' he is armed wid two revolvers … (*to his Harry phone*) Harry are you there, can you hear me Harry? Harry?

Tracy I am certainly not Mr James and I am not familiar with the term 'taking the piss' … you wish to speak with Hamish … well …

She looks across at Ray who indicates that he does not wish to impersonate a Scottish cultural figure. He is on the line to Harry.

Ray If you insist on going in there Harry, go in fighting … let her see you are not beaten Harry, don't let her mash you up –

Tracy I'm afraid he *can't* get to the phone right now …

Ray breaks into African on the other line.

Ray Spittin' and screamin' dis is ver' bad, ah would advise you to close de doors and windows and not let de man in … tell him to go to his office …

Tracy How about our executive producer Gunther Schlondorf … yes he is from Dusseldorf …

Ray Tell her what you fucking think of her Harry –

Tracy Gunther –

Ray Maclellan no –

Tracy Gunther –

She holds the phone out to him. He has no choice. With three lines already in his hands he does a Nazi-style German accent into Tracy's phone.

Ray Hullo Mr James – here is Gunther Schlondorf from zer *Hamish MacHeggarty Show* … ja, ja, naturlich ve are interested in … er …

Tracy (*hisses*) Dave Hewitt.

Ray Zer David Hewitt.

Tracy Is he free tomorrow – the 25th?

Ray Is he free tomorrow – zer twvnty-funfth? (*Moves to his other line.*) Don't ring the bell Harry don't ring the bell don't – (*to African*) Answer it Missy Harrod. Do not let dis man in. Ah am sure you have t'ings to say to him but – (*to James*) Ve vish to record a conversation with Mr Hewitt undt Mr MacHeggarty –

41

Tracy In London. We record the show in London.

Ray (*hisses briefly at Tracy*) Why are you doing this Maclellan? (*then to Peter James*) No zere is no one here called Maclellan zere is just the team of zer *Hamish MacHeggarty Show*, zere is Claudia –

Tracy Hi!

Ray Also is Siobhan –

Tracy Top a' the mornin' ter yer!

He loses his cool on the line to Mrs Harrod.

Ray A real disaster Missy Harrod on de hands, do not let de man in … (*as Gunther*) And also ve hev – (*switching phone again*) Harry do not go in there do not for Christ's sake … (*He has said this to Harry's ex-wife. He stops, appalled, and changes phones so that he says the next line to Harry.*) Ah am warnin' you Missy Harrod –

Harry must be expressing some puzzlement at the fact that an African is talking to him.

Dis is Kwame Obolonga of de Alcoholics Anonymous I am t'inkin' we are havin' de cross line heah sir who is you … ?

Tracy Good fucking question.

Ray (*now totally confused about which phone is which. He picks up the phone to the ex-wife.*) Don't do it Harry, for Christ's sake, don't go in there, she will eat you alive –

Tracy is signalling that he is on the wrong call. He picks up another phone and speaks in his own voice.

Harry, it's me Harry, I am talking to that prick of an agent, Harry we are going to claw this one back, Harry don't do it for the sake of the *Harry Harrod* –

He stops. Appalled. In the confusion he has said all this

*into the wrong phone. To Hewitt's agent. Tracy mimes
that this is so.*

Hullo … is that Peter James … Peter … hi this is Ray
Goodenough here from the *Harry Harrod Show* … Harry
is … you recognized my voice? Well Peter you're a hard
man to get to talk to and we were having a little … you
know … right … right … look I suppose it worked in one
sense Peter because we are having a conversation about
your client and you are a hard man to get to Peter and …
we were kidding sure but … all I wanted to find out was
you know why your client who had agreed, who had
agreed to …

Tracy Ray –

Ray To appear on the *Harry Harrod Show* had decided it
was not for him … I simply wished to have a conversation
to see if there was any leeway on this and if so how we
might … listen Peter, the *Harry Harrod Show* is not to
everyone's taste, there are times when I find it a touch vulgar … sure more than a touch but … I don't think it is
fair or helpful to describe it as you have done …

Tracy Ray –

Ray Well 'piece of poop' is a harsh thing to … well you
have a right to that opinion, I do not wish to burn our
bridges Mr James, I think there is still room for dialogue
… do not say that Mr James, please do not say that about
the *Harry Harrod Show*, I beseech you do not …

Tracy Ray –

Ray 'Vomit' is a harsh thing to say about something that
is basically a piece of entertainment and is not to be …
what have you done, Mr James, that entitles you to make
such a remark?

Tracy is listening to the other three phones, all dead, as

43

Ray winds up on the line.

Tracy Ray please – Harry has gone in there. We have to get to him. We have to ring June, we have to ring his mobile Ray, if she gets started on him Ray, we will never see Harry Harrod again, there will not *be* any studio, never mind Dave Hewitt, never mind –

Ray I'll tell you what you've done. You've sat in an office and you've sat on your poofy little arse and made money out of a load of half-baked teenagers with less talent in their whole *body* than Harry Harrod has in his little fingers and ... oh you are a horrible little fucking queer aren't you?

Tracy Ray please –

Ray You are a loathsome little paedophiliac arse-licking cunting little shitbag who couldn't cross the street without his mother showed him the way and who has never done anything of interest in his miserable little sodomitic life because – (*He is really going. He climbs up on the desk.*) No you listen to me you *cunt*, you listen to Ray fucking Goodenough, I do not care if your turdy little wanker David 'Never-Even-Had-a-Hit-in-Finland' Hewitt falls under a bus on his way to get his next three hundred grammes of uncut heroin or whatever it is that gets him through the day, while you sit there in your ponytail pretending to have a sense of rhythm, I am sure you *do* have a ponytail you little *cunt*, I do not care if none of your clients ever appear on the *Harry Harrod Show* ... how *fucking dare you say that about the show you cunt* ... I will come round there and I will kill you, I will kill you, but slowly I will – (*He is apoplectic with fury. Stops. Looks down at phone.*) He hung up.

Tracy That is his democratic right. He doesn't have to listen to you Ray.

Ray He does. Call him back.

Tracy No.

Ray sits. Puts his head in his hands.

Ray Our boy is in there. With his ex-wife. Drunk. No one will take our calls. What are we doing here Maclellan?

Tracy I'll call his mobile.

Ray Call your mother.

Tracy Not when you're in the room.

Ray I'm not in the room.

Tracy What's that thing on the desk? Like an old Jewish tramp? Isn't that Ray Goodenough?

Ray gets up.

Ray I'm going. I'm going to walk the corridor. Phone your mother. (*He walks towards the door. Stops when he gets there.*) What's with this letter Maclellan? You after another job or what?

Tracy What makes you think that?

Ray You leaving me Maclellan? You had enough of Ray Goodenough?

Tracy Why ever would you think that?

Ray Phone your mother. I'm leaving. Phone your mother.

And he goes out into the corridor. Tracy picks up a phone.

Tracy Mother ... it's Tracy ... did that letter ... it did ... well look Mother would you do me a favour ... I want you to open it ... could you do that ... and read it to me ... (*She yawns.*) But not now because Ray is listening in to this conversation. Just read it and get a good idea of what's in it and I will call you back when he is not listening. Bye.

Shame-faced, Ray comes back into the office.

Ray Why would you want another job? What are you missing out on here?

Tracy Scenery. Real men.

Ray I'm a real man. Where it counts.

Tracy Yeah?

This joke is a touch too near the truth to be funny. Ray looks away. Tracy becomes suddenly affectionate.

Tracy I'll call Harry. What is the matter with him? (*She is dialling.*)

Ray Tracy –

Tracy What?

Ray Am I a bad person?

Tracy What do you think?

Ray Why is it so important to me? Why is David Hewitt so important to me?

Tracy Why is anything important? Why do we think something is filling our horizon and then look back on it and say 'Well. What was all *that* about.' (*She has got through.*) 'The vodaphone number you are calling has been switched off.' (*She shrugs.*) It's life I suppose. Such a small thing, but it animates us like puppets – 'I'm in love! I'm angry! I'm dying!'

Ray You have got another job. You're sounding suspiciously upmarket.

46

Tracy I don't know why we get so worked up about things. I haven't the faintest idea why I stay here for example. I mean I could do anything. Couldn't I?

Ray You could retire.

Tracy I could retire. To the Lake District. I'd like that. Wouldn't I?

Ray No.

Tracy You know me so well Mr Goodenough don't you?

Ray No.

Tracy No. No you don't.

Ray puts his feet up on the desk.

Ray Do you remember that guy with the alligator? That got out in the studio? And nearly bit Elton John?

Tracy We never had Elton John.

Ray I mean this room has seen so much, you know? So many really *famous* people have been through this room, you know? And sat here talking about their lives and being witty and clever or tragic and important, you know?

Tracy And sometimes plain dull. (*She starts to dial.*) Famous people are just like you or me Ray. They run around and make important noises for a while and then they die. It's no big deal.

Ray If I thought that I wouldn't be here.

Tracy looks at him with great fondness.

Tracy No. No you wouldn't. (*And speaks into the phone.*) Harry you're back … where are you Harry … ? Harry you're out of there …

Ray Let me talk to him …

Tracy Call him on his other mobile … Harry where are you … in a taxi Harry, that was quick … she … what did she do to you Harry? (*She covers the phone. To Ray*) She said something to him. He's in bits.

Ray has been dialling.

That's Ray, Harry, on your other line, answer Harry, talk to him Harry … because he cares Harry, and because you need to talk to people who care … people who love you Harry … Harry I know she doesn't love you, that's why you got divorced, remember? Answer the phone Harry …

And Ray gives a big grin.

Ray Harry, it's Ray here, it's Ray your producer who loves you and thinks you're great. Harry I am here, I am in your right ear …

Tracy (*covering her mouthpiece with her hand*) Stop sweet-talking him and get him over here.

Ray (*to his phone*) She said would I stop sweet-talking you and get you over here. (*To Tracy, putting his hand over the mouthpiece.*) Don't put your hand over the mouthpiece. He feels excluded.

Tracy (*talks to her phone*) He told me not to put my hand over the mouthpiece. Apparently you feel excluded.

Ray Pay the driver, Harry you mustn't pay the driver, tell him to take you to the office, it can't be far Harry, Harry where are you, Harry don't do …

Tracy Anything stupid, will you Harry, you don't want to die Harry, you don't want to die, life is good Harry, life is very, very sweet, you mustn't –

Ray Give up Harry, you mustn't be negative Harry, you

must be positive, where are you Harry, you sound like you are –

Tracy By a river Harry. Did I hear water Harry, did I hear seagulls? I swear I heard a foghorn Harry, Harry are you going into a –

Ray Building. Yes Harry, I hear that, I hear that, is it your flats Harry, is that where you are going? You're not going back to see June are you Harry, or to see –

Tracy Sarah? Or Tabitha? Don't go and see Tabitha Harry, if it's Tabitha, turn right around from that building and walk straight out of there –

Ray It sounds like you are getting in a lift –

Tracy In a lift Harry, Harry don't do anything silly –

Ray Like jumping out of a window Harry, don't jump out of a window Harry, for Christ's sake don't –

Tracy has covered her mouthpiece.

Tracy Don't put ideas into his head you jerk. He's going up in a *lift* and you're practically *ordering* him to jump out of a window.

Ray She's saying that I shouldn't put the idea of suicide into your mind and give you the idea that, you know, jumping out of a window would be a good idea ... I don't think it is a good idea Harry ... Harry ...

Tracy Harry listen to me – (*This, as she takes her hand off the mouthpiece.*) Where are you Harry? Where are you going Harry? What are you going to do Harry? Why did you go up in the lift Harry? Tell us what you are feeling Harry, will you? What are you scared of Harry?

Both Ray and Tracy are listening very intently to their phones. As they do so **Harry Harrod**, *a once good-*

*looking man in his late fifties, in a smart suit, comes in
from the back very quietly. So absorbed are they that at
first they don't realize he is in the room and crouch
down gluing their ears to the phones to catch his quiet
speech.*

Harry I'm scared of work. I'm scared of not having
work. I'm scared of people. I'm scared of noise. I'm
scared of silence. I'm scared of my friends. I'm scared of
my enemies. I'm scared of living. I'm scared of dying.

*Very slowly Ray and Tracy turn, realizing that he is in
the room with them.*

Ray Why did you do that Harry? Why did you scare me
like that Harry? Why didn't you let us know you were
here Harry?

Harry just stares ahead of him.

Can't you talk to a person?

*Tracy and Ray stand watching him. Very slowly Tracy
puts her phone back on the hook. Ray disconnects his.
Harry just stands there.*
  Blackout.

Act Two

As at the end of Act One. Harry is standing staring in front of him. He doesn't answer.

Ray Harry I hate to have to say this but in some ways you were more fun at the end of a phone.

Tracy Harry –

Ray Don't upset the guy Maclellan –

Tracy Harry I never knew you had a son.

Harry No.

Ray Can we think positive here Maclellan? Can we look on the bright side? (*He moves to Harry.*) Harry, we have to be positive about this Harry. We are getting things together here Harry. I have been on the phone to Dave Hewitt's agent. He said I was a foul-mouthed little half-witted lecherous motherfucking son of a Jewish scumbag but we are *talking* Harry. That has to be good.

Harry doesn't answer. He goes to sit down. Pause. Harry sits.

Tracy Harry –

Ray Can we not sit around weeping please? Can we get on and be doing here please?

Harry I'm finished Ray. I'm all through.

Ray Harry you are one of the most important people in British television. You are a landmark Harry. You are a benchmark. You are a benchmark and a landmark. You are also a hallmark Harry. You are sterling. You have been in television for twenty years. Do you know what that signifies Harry? Do you know what twenty years *is* Harry?

Harry puts his head in his hands.

Harry Twenty years is too long.

Tracy Harry. Is your son –

Ray Can we concentrate on the job in hand Maclellan? Can we start putting this thing to bed here please? Can we start to *work* Maclellan please?

Harry I'm finished Ray. I'm all through.

Ray Harry you have very nearly won, you *should have* won, major industry awards.

Harry is close to being sick.

You are a mensch Harry. Do you know what that word means Harry? In Yiddish, Harry, a language with which I am entirely unacquainted, on account I am an assimilated uncultured rubbish Jew from Hendon who thinks a yarmulke is a kind of motorbike, in Yiddish Harry a *mensch* is a kind of …

Harry I know what a mensch is Ray. You told me.

Ray You are the presenter and editor of the *Harry Harrod Show* Harry. And you have been insulted. Some horrible little, clammy little, half-assed cunt-licking bum-banger of a so-called agent has *persuaded* a Mr David Hewitt that your show is somehow or other *beneath his dignity* … you're laughing Harry but unbelievable as it may seem that is how they have tried to insult you today but we are *not going to give in* Harry.

Harry lifts his head and stares blearily at Ray.

Harry Why not?

Ray laughs.

Ray 'Why not?' Doncha love the guy? Doncha love the sensayuma? (*suddenly serious*) Because it matters Harry. Because it counts.

Harry Why does it count?

Ray Isn't he perfect? Isn't he the bees' knees? 'Why does it count?' He's Descartes. He's Spinoza. He's A. J. Ayer. 'Why does it count?' I don't know why it counts Harry. But I am telling you that it counts. And that you are now going to call Mr *Peter James*, the perverted drone who steals ten per cent of the appalling little no talent slob *Hewitt*, who nonetheless, when he has been dignified by a conversation in the presence of you mein Fuehrer, mein Freund, will be a sparkling jewel in the sky and you are going to talk him back on to the show.

Tracy You never talked about any son Harry. We never even knew you had a son.

Harry I would prefer not.

Ray laughs. Looks round at the office.

Ray Is the guy putting me on? He would 'prefer not'. My God Harry!

Tracy Ray. What is it with you?

But Ray has started to dial.

Ray All we need to do Harry is get this guy back. Harry we are in bad with his agent.

Harry We are in bad with all the agents.

Ray Harry we have done terrible things here today. We have impersonated Negroes. We have pretended to be

Scottish, Harry. We most probably will be arrested for what we have done. (*Ray has not got through.*) You have to talk to the agent Harry.

Tracy Ray –

Ray Will you stop criticizing me? Will you leave me alone? Do you think I don't love this man? Do you think I don't know best? (*intense, to Harry*) James will not give Hewitt's number to just anyone. You are one of the few people in the *world* to whom he might entrust it.

Harry I'm not so sure.

Ray I'm dialling. Are you dialling Maclellan?

Wearily, Tracy starts to dial.

Who are you dialling?

Tracy My mother.

Ray What's with your mother all of a sudden? Is she going to get us out of this crisis? Does she have an in to the music business? (*His call to James is ringing.*) It is ringing Harry. We have tone. (*He moves towards him with the phone.*) You were an artist of the phone call Harry. Remember? 'Let me sit at your feet!' you used to say and your voice came over the wires and it was like it managed to hypnotize those musicians and dancers and actors and politicians. 'Let me sit at your feet!' And you'd sort of swoon into the receiver like it was a living thing Harry, until I could imagine you wriggling out at the other end like a genie out of a bottle.

Tracy Mother … it's Tracy … yes … that letter … did you read it … ?

Ray Would you listen to her Harry? At a time like this what is she doing? Is she phoning her mother or is she phoning her mother?

Tracy She's phoning her mother. (*to the phone*) Yes … that's it … it doesn't matter if you don't quite get it, just *read* it OK … ?

Ray Maybe they know it's me Harry. Maybe they sense it's my ring. Maybe you should hold the phone. No?

Harry just looks at him bleakly. Then a moment of excitement. Ray holds the mouthpiece to Harry's face.

Harry. You are through. Talk to the people.

Tracy No, no, Mother it is not that one Mother … I know the drain in the back garden looks important but it isn't that one … when I said official I meant …

She looks around in a somewhat paranoid fashion. Ray takes the phone away from Harry. Listens to what is going on at the other end. Looks paranoid. Holds it back to Harry's mouth. Harry doesn't speak.

You know … official … I couldn't call because … if you wouldn't mind going down, bring up all the letters that are there and read them … I don't get any personal mail Mother … because I don't have any personal life …

Ray Because of you Mother.

Tracy Mother I am asking you to do it OK? This is an important letter OK?

Her voice is raised. Ray shoots a quick, worried glance. It is hard to tell whether this is concern for Tracy or for the business in hand. Meanwhile he has listened to the phone again and realized that Mrs Parker must have disconnected. Very rapidly he dials again.

Ray Can you keep the noise down please? The boss is about to speak. We are about to re-connect him.

And like a mother tempting a child to eat, Ray holds

the phone to Harry's mouth. Harry just looks at it. Ray panics. He puts his hand over his nose and speaks to the agent.

Could you hold the line please? (*And he holds the receiver back to Harry's mouth. Whispers*) Speak to them Harry.

Harry I would prefer not.

And he disconnects the phone. Ray goes absolutely wild.

Ray All we need is the number Harry. We are almost there with this. All we need is one lousy number Harry. All we need is David Hewitt's number.

Tracy I said I would hold and I will hold OK. Mother … yes I will hold … (*She puts the phone down on the desk.*)

Ray Thanks for your help Maclellan.

Tracy No trouble.

Ray Personal calls in office hours.

Tracy I know. But hell. It was about my mastectomy. I thought that would almost justify it.

Ray You think your having your tits sawn off is as important as finding a *home number* for Mr Dave Hewitt?

Tracy How could I possibly think that?

Ray Leave your problems at home. Don't bring them into the workplace.

Tracy I left my tits at home didn't I?

Ray Of course you did, we've all the tits we need on the *Harry Harrod Show*. I am going to dial this scumbag James one more time Harry. And this time you are going to talk to him.

Harry does not answer.

I am going to force you to talk Harry. I am going to make you do this. (*to Tracy*) You. Dial Mrs Parker.

Tracy You have to be joking.

Ray Make her put Harry through to Peter James.

Tracy And how in God's name do I do that?

Harry gives a self-pitying laugh. Embittered.

Harry Tell her I'm a big hit in America.

Pause. Tracy starts to dial. Ray is suddenly worried.

Ray What are you doing Maclellan?

Tracy Calling Mrs Parker to get her to put Harry through to Peter James so as we can get Dave Hewitt's number.

Ray No Africans.

Tracy No Africans.

Ray No Scottish. Please no Scottish.

Harry She won't put you through. I am no longer a name to conjure with Tracy.

Tracy's line to Mrs Parker is ringing.

Tracy (*to Ray*) You know what Ray?

Ray What?

Tracy It was you who always said 'Let me sit at your feet!' Not Harry.

Ray Do not rewrite history Maclellan. And no Welsh. No Irish. No East Anglian. No German. No Spanish. No –

But Tracy is already through to Mrs Parker. And doing a very credible West Coast American. Both Harry and

Ray goggle at her.

Tracy Hullo is that the Peter James Agency in London, this is Lucy Pfefferman of Pfefferman Media in Los Angeles, California we are working here on the media launch of the … (*The first name that occurs to her.*) *Harry Harrod Show* …

Panic from all concerned.

… over here … well our understanding is that Mr Harrod is talking to two major networks and that CBS are very hot on the show … you are … ? Well Mrs Parker … (*She gives a light laugh.*) People are going to love the guy with the severed penis Mrs Parker … you … you surprise me Mrs Parker, people over here are *very* excited about this show, you … you'll put me through to Mr James, you are so kind … (*to her mother*) Mother … ? Are you there … ? Mother?

Harry What has all this got to do with Dave Hewitt?

Tracy Hi! Peter! You are Peter James? This is Lucy Pfefferman from Pfefferman Media in Los Angeles, California, we are handling the media on the launch of the *Harry Harrod Show* … yes there's a lot of interest over here … well it was Harry Harrod himself who said I should call you Peter because … well he is right here beside me Peter as we speak …

Harry You what?

Ray Get over there …

Tracy He is here with us and it was he who told me to call …

Harry For God's sake Tracy!

Ray Get over there and talk!

Tracy Sure he will speak with you Peter!

Harry Tracy –

But she has handed him the phone.

Ray Talk!

Harry Hi!

Ray Talk more!

Harry Hi!

Ray Talk even more!

Harry Hi Peter! … well I'm in … er …

Tracy Los Angeles!

Harry Los Angeles … and … er … it's …

Ray Hot.

Harry Hot … and there are … you know …

Tracy Palm trees.

Harry Palm trees. A lot of palm trees … Why did I get Lucy to call you Peter? Well … (*forced laugh*)

Ray CBS love the show …

Harry CBS love the show …

Ray (*turns to Tracy*) This is like being in the studio. With him on talkback. And me right behind him. Isn't it?

Tracy Sssh!

Harry Who at CBS loves the show … well that's a very good question … it's …

Ray Alan Finkielkraut. In Chicago.

Harry Alan Finkielkraut. In Chicago. He responded well

to the show, and … you see I wondered whether …

Tracy Dave Hewitt …

Harry I was thinking of Dave. And American exposure would … you know … be good for Dave … I mean I understand Dave has a problem with the show but this might …

Tracy *That's* the idea …

Harry You think it might … well that's great, I … but you'd just like to call – (*Horror. He puts his hand over the phone. To Ray and Tracy*) He wants to call this Finkielkraut guy in Chicago. Now.

Tracy Tell him that will not be necessary.

Harry Peter that will not be necessary. (*to Tracy*) Why will it not be necessary?

Tracy Finkielkraut is calling him.

Harry How do I know Finkielkraut is calling him?

Ray Harry use initiative. Do we have to talk you through every move you make? Are we your production team or an intensive care unit?

Harry Well Peter, Alan said he was going to call you about, what time do you have in London now … ? Six … ? Well he said he'd call around lunchtime his time which would be around now your time. I don't know what time it is here, I don't have a watch … look I need to ask you about Dave Hewitt's appearance on the London show.

Ray That's better.

Tracy has been dialling the agency.

Tracy (*deep South accent*) Hullo Peter James Agency, this is Elly Mae Jackson from the offices of Alan Finkielkraut of CBS television in Chicago ...

Harry I'm sorry Peter.

Tracy Mr Finkielkraut wishes to speak with Mr James concerning a client of yours ... a Mr David Hewitt, it is most urgent ... you will try to break into his call? (*She rounds on Harry who is being earbashed by James.*)

Ray Get Hewitt's number!

Tracy checks on her mother phone.

Tracy Mother was that you? (*She whistles down the line.*)

Harry Peter I quite understand why Dave Hewitt should not want to do the show ... I suppose ... well ... my people in London were getting a little anxious ... Ray Goodenough the producer ... he was ... he can be you know ... yes he is a foul-mouthed individual ...

Ray 'Foul-mouthed individual!' That's beautiful.

Harry Look Ray is ... well he's past his best he is ... a very, very difficult person to work with I agree ...

Ray 'Very very difficult!' This is Olivier we are looking at here! This is Tom Hanks! This is world-class acting!

Harry Alan Finkielkraut is on the line for you now, you say? Well Peter, talk to him, give him my love, give my love to Chicago ...

Tracy Yes I am putting Mr Finkielkraut on now ...

And Ray comes on her phone as Finkielkraut. A very smooth American.

Ray Hi, Peter James? This is Alan Finkielkraut in Chicago ... what time is it here ... ? Well it's er ... a little later than it is in LA ha, ha, ha, and it's ... snowing can you beat that? Yeah well that's great Peter just great ...

look we wanted to talk with you because between you and me there is considerable excitement on the network about this … *Harry Harrod Show* and Harry was telling me about one of your clients, a Mr David Hewitt … sure, sure … well I just wanted to reassure you Mr James that that is *exactly* the sort of person we are looking for over here, kinda young, kinda new, kinda *weird* … you have Harry on the other line! Hey talk to him, give him my best! I'll hold! (*to Harry as Peter James switches calls*) Get the number. Now.

Harry Peter hi! … well I am glad you talked with Alan, we are constantly in touch, I'll be talking to him very soon and … look listen here's an idea for you, let me call Dave Hewitt, Peter, and put this to him, you are very kind … a home number and a mobile number … right, right … I have those Peter I'll call him on my way to the airport. (*calling*) Have a nice day!

Ray Call him. Now.

Harry Ray – why am I doing this?

Tracy Christ! *I'll* call him!

> *She grabs the numbers off Harry as Harry sits heavily. Deflated.*

Harry There's no point anyway because –

> *Ray is on.*

Ray (*as Finkielkraut*) Hi Peter, well that's great, I am surprised the show has had problems at the London end, we loved the whole thing, the guy with the penis especially and … sure it was the *producer* was a problem you think … look when we take the show we will lose him, we buy 'em and sell 'em Peter …

Tracy The home number is engaged.

Ray Harry ring the mobile. Harry what is up with you today? (*back as Finkielkraut*) Derogatory language? Well I kind of hate that Peter, I like to think that even in an extreme situation I would not resort to de … look if Harry wants to dump this asshole Goodenough let him do so, we … is that right? (*to Harry*) Apparently Harry, you hate me Harry. Apparently you have been trying to dump me for years. Doncha love this Peter James guy? (*back on to James*) Go on to me about this Goodenough guy Peter, I love to hear your views on him Peter –

Tracy Ray get off the line. We have the numbers now. Get off the line. (*to her mother*) Mother? (*to Harry*) The home number is still engaged. Harry will you dial Hewitt's mobile? Please?

Ray Look I am Jewish myself Mr James and there are those of us who let the side down and this guy sounds like one of them … 'a poisonous little Jewish dwarf …' well Peter …

Tracy Ray get off the line!

Ray This Ray Goodenough is the guy who screwed up the *Harry Harrod Show*, well that is real interesting Mr James, that is useful to hear, although I do not quite see how a … (*Slowly his voice undergoes a sea change. From Finkielkraut to Ray.*) … how a *producer* can screw up a show when he is the guy doing all the work. No this is me Mr James this is Ray Goodenough the quote 'poisonous little Jewish dwarf' unquote, no I am not in Chicago or LA and neither is my *good friend* Harry Harrod who is very far from being washed up you little *cunt*, my God how I hate you, but is right next to me in the office laughing at you, you poofy little pigeon-chested tiny-dicked shit-flavoured son of a bumbanging shirtlifter *ha!* … *ha!* … It is you who will never work again you anti-semitic arsehole … you are … excuse me you are an anti-semite, I can smell

63

it coming down out of the phone, a sewerful of Nazi lies and Jew-hating filth, you turd-brained cold-hearted greedy little philistine *cunt*, yes we will ring Hewitt, we will ring him and torment him, we will ring him at four in the morning and breathe down his phone or worse still we will ring him and be nice to him and find that you have *completely and utterly misrepresented his position* ... of course we haven't sold the show to CBS you credulous little arsehole, no one in their right minds would buy this show, Border Television wouldn't cross the road to spit at it ... (*to Harry*) Dial Hewitt. Before he can get to him.

Harry Ray ... something has happened ...

Ray Dial you spineless cunt! Dial Hewitt on both lines!

Tracy Mother is that you?

Ray And Tracy, call in to James's office on all his lines. He must not be allowed to talk to Hewitt before we do. (*to his James phone*) Rant on, rant on, you pathetic little man, rant on!

Tracy African? Scottish? Greek?

Ray Who cares? Harry dial Hewitt!

Harry You have to listen to what I have to say.

Ray When you've dialled!

Tracy is dialling into James's office. Harry too starts to dial Hewitt's home number.

Both numbers. Home number and mobile!

Tracy Hullo, this is Hermione Diller, I'm a singer-songwriter. I am waiting to speak with Mr James. I have a song ... (*She sings, folky.*) 'The leaves of autumn are on Doolnachin Bay ...' (*As she is singing she is dialling in on another line.*)

Ray What are you doing?

Tracy I'm singing.

Ray is still being earbashed by Peter James. And Tracy is through on her next call into the James's office. This time a very no-nonsense posh lady.

Hullo, is that the office of Peter James. I am Sally Nolan from the Taunton solicitors Nolan, Nolan and, er, Nolan and I am ringing on behalf of a client of ours who alleges she has been assaulted by Mr James in a hotel in Taunton in January 1992, do you have our letter? (*While she has been doing this she has been dialling the next call in. It starts to ring as she finishes.*) Do take your other call ...

Ray ... No, you will die, you odious little deformed *agent*, you will die horribly, you will die screaming ...

Tracy (*talking on her next call*) Hullo, here is der Dutch Guild of Freelance Film Agents. I ring for Mr Peter James from Omshterdom, it is imperative I shpeak wid him ...

Ray That's it, isn't it? You are scared we are going to talk to him because he likes the show doesn't he ... ?

Harry Home number's engaged. Mobile's engaged.

Ray (*laughs down his phone*) Rant on, rant on, I am not impressed ... call me a fucking cunt, I do not care ... rant on, rant on ...

Tracy Hullo this is Aer Lingus. I'm after contacting a Mr Peter James ...

Ray Listen you will die alone and afraid in some bedsitting room and your agency will die with you and no one will remember you and dogs will come and urinate on your grave and I myself will lower my trousers and do a horrible Jewish dump all over your unmarked last resting place, you will die with my curse on you, *cunt*, you will die because I say so! (*He stops. In genuine surprise.*) He hung up! Just as it was getting good! Get *through* to him Maclellan before he can tell his office to get Hewitt.

Tracy I have quite a few calls into him already.

Ray Harry you take the mobile, I'll try the home number. Keep dialling for Christ's sake!

Tracy is connected on her latest call.

Tracy (*to Ray*) Five. Which one will he take?

Ray I don't care so long as he takes one.

Tracy (*to Mrs Parker*) Good afternoon I am ringing from the offices of the Inland Revenue in Newcastle and I wish to speak with Mr Peter James *urgently* … he is on another call … he has several urgent calls …

As she is put through, Harry is dialling the home number. Harry is still dialling the mobile. She turns to the office.

She's putting Nolan through … yes …

Ray Who the fuck is Nolan?

Tracy Nolan is a wonderful woman …

Ray (*very excited*) It's ringing! I have ringing tone! I have ringing tone on Hewitt's home number!

Harry The mobile is still engaged!

Tracy Thank you so much … (*almost to herself*) How I loathe you Mrs Parker. (*change to Sally Nolan*) Hullo there Mr James, this is Sally Nolan … we've been in correspondence with you concerning a *woman who alleges you assaulted her in a hotel in Taunton Mr* … this is a serious matter and even though this young woman is schizophrenic she still …

Ray I have tone! I still have tone! Harry do you have tone, Harry? Do you have tone on the mobile? (*He grabs the phone off Harry.*) You're not dialling it right. Who are you calling?

Harry Hewitt's mobile.

Ray I'll dial the mobile. I'm through on the home phone but no answer. Suppose …

Harry What?

Ray Suppose he's in the car, my God, he may be in the car, do we have the car number?

Tracy No.

Ray (*he is through*) I am through Maclellan … (*very charming suddenly*) Hullo there, is that the Hewitt residence? (*very slowly, as to a foreigner*) Do you speak English? I am calling for Mr David Hewitt … well may I speak with Mrs Hewitt … er Ingeborg?

Tracy You don't need to ask your assistant for the letter … Mr James (*to Mrs Parker, as she dials another number*) 'Long ago in Lagavulin …' dish is Omshterdom calling … hullo is anyone there, this is the Inland Revenue speaking … hullo this is Aer Lingus for Mr Peter James …

Ray (*to Tracy*) Keep up the pressure. Until I have Hewitt on the line, keep up the pressure.

Tracy 'ullo Jeannie I think we got a crossed line … (*And is through on the other line. This time she is Spanish.*) Hullo, hullo, here is Las Palabras Musicales in Barcelona …

Ray (*to the Hewitt residence*) Mrs Hewitt, hullo I wanted to speak with your husband Mrs Hewitt, with Mr Hewitt, this is, who am I? I am … well my name is Goodenough Mrs Hewitt … and Pete, Pete James gave me your number …

Tracy It is not my fault if all your assistant's lines are busy, I am a *solicitor* Mr James ... please do not shout at me ...

Ray (*on his call*) He went out in the car Mrs Hewitt ... there's a phone there ... ? You, do you have that number ... ? *Marvellous* I'll call him in the car, Mrs Hewitt thank you for that number ... (*Puts hand over mouthpiece, as he writes down number and dials.*) He went out in the car. Apparently he is depressed.

Tracy (*as Nolan*) I very much doubt it ...

Ray holds the other phone to his ear. He has dialled Hewitt's car on this one. Winces into first phone. Clearly getting an ear bashing from Hewitt femme.

Ray His dog died. Big deal. Car number's engaged. Dial the mobile Harry. Dial the mobile. Aren't you through on the mobile?

Harry has been dialling. But it is as if each digit is a great weight. He rests between each one.

Harry It's still engaged.

Tracy I beg your pardon ...

Ray I realize that Mrs Hewitt, I love dogs, I love them and just because they have four legs doesn't mean they are ...

Tracy How dare you ...

Ray ... they are cleverer than some humans sure Mrs ... well it's been great talking to you ... (*to Tracy*) I have tone on the carphone Maclellan, I have tone on the carphone, we are almost there just hold on to Mr James ... (*to Mrs Hewitt*) Well bye bye and ...

Tracy Now look here ...

Ray I'll think about Mufty, Mrs Hewitt, he sounded a great little, dachsunds are full of character indeed, good-bye …

Tracy I am sorry you have an urgent call to make Mr James but this young woman is alleging you beat her with a lavatory brush in room 5601 … Listen Mr James –

Ray has got through.

Ray Hullo … is that Dave Hewitt … it is … hi Mr Hewitt my name is Ray Goodenough and …

Tracy How dare you …

Ray Sure, Ray Goodenough, your name and number were given to me by your agent Peter James … I am an old friend of his and well … he trusts me … the *Harry Harrod Show* …

Tracy has been getting a mouthful from the unfortunate Mr James who is by now on the verge of a nervous breakdown. Tracy switches to her real voice, into both phones at the same time.

Tracy Mr James you can shout at me all you like and if you want to know, I do not give a stuff about you …

Ray You can pack it in now Maclellan.

Tracy I am Tracy Maclellan and I work for Mr Ray Goodenough. Yes Mr James. That excellent and informative programme.

Ray Look, I'm sorry you feel that Dave …

Tracy Yes I am Sally Nolan and I am also all the other people who have been clogging your switchboard …

Ray I know what you mean Dave … some of us have to work on it …

Tracy's voice rises.

Tracy You can send all the lawyers you like, you horrible little queer, we are not afraid of you on the *Harry Harrod Show* ...

Ray Well ...

Tracy No we're not, you rude bastard and if you want to know I used to be a professional actress and this is just the beginning of a lifetime of persecution because we never forgive on the *Harry Harrod Show*. And – (*She picks up the phone to her mother.*) I've almost finished Mother, I'll be right with you. (*back to the unfortunate agent*) Fuck you up your arse if you have one you shirt-lifting scumbag, fuck you very much! (*And into some Mrs Parker phones.*) And fuck you too, you old bag! Haddaway and shite! (*She slams the phones down.*)

Ray is talking to Hewitt. Very, very reasonable.

Ray No, sure, sure ... it was just that Peter had a little re-think and was very, very keen for you to come on the show ... yes, yes he did ... that was why he gave me your number ... (*slightly forced laugh*) I don't think it means he thinks your career is on the slide Dave, I just think ... Dave, Dave, Dave, Dave, let me sit at your feet, will you do that ... ? Let me sit at your feet.

It seems to be working. The old magic. Tracy, who has given up momentarily, looks across at him.

Tracy Ray –

Ray Well why don't you just talk to me and see if you trust me ... let's talk ... sure let's get to trust each other and talk about the quote 'chat show from hell' unquote ...

Tracy Don't talk about the show, Ray! It upsets you!

Ray There are things wrong with it sure ... They what ...

70

what ... ? They what? (Something Dave has said has freaked him. He turns to Harry.) He says he has heard they are going to pull the show Harry. Can you believe that? Can you credit that Harry?

Harry Where did he hear that?

Ray Dave where did you hear ... *(He refuses to believe such a thing.)* All over. All over. Doncha love it?

Tracy has realized that she is still on the line to her mother. She picks it up very tentatively.

Tracy Mother ... are you still there ... ? I am sorry it's ... sure ... sure ... that'll be the one ... *(She seems suddenly tired.)* Sure, you better read it to me ...

Ray *(swooning into the mouthpiece)* I just wanted to talk about you really because whatever you may think your agent thinks, I am a *big fan* ... *(to Tracy)* I want more dope on Hewitt. Now. Titles of records. All that shit. Weren't you going to have it faxed over?

Tracy I'm on the line to my mother!

Ray Your mother? At a time like this? You are calling your mother?

Tracy goes to her mother phone.

Tracy Just hold it there could you ... ? Hold on a minute ... Just hang on could you?

Ray Your own songs ... well I don't have a favourite exactly, except they are *all* my favourite Dave ...

Tracy Library it's Tracy here from the *Harry Harrod Show* ... about that fax about Dave Hewitt ... great thanks.

Ray Well you have a quality of ... well ... *stillness* I'd call it ... it's like you have a very *still centre* ... *(to Harry)*

Keep dialling the mobile. Maclellan, I need facts. I am flying blind here.

But Tracy is having problems.

Tracy It's on its way …

Ray (*on the phone to Hewitt*) What specific tracks … ?
Well it's more as I say, more of a *feeling* that emanates
from your whole oeuvre than one specific song or album
although … I appreciate that … I appreciate … you are
surrounded by liars and flatterers … (*He puts his hand
over the mouthpiece.*) He is lucky to get such people to
put up with him. He is an unbelievable loser! Harry?

Harry It's still engaged.

Ray Who is he talking to? How is he managing to talk to
someone at the *same* time as me? Are we dealing with
another *artist* of the mobile telephone here? Where is this
fax? Where is this fax?

*Tracy has been engaged with the machine. Squinting at
the paper as it rolls out.*

Tracy His last album was called *Moon in the Bangkok
Hilton*.

Ray (*talks into phone*) Take *Moon in the Bangkok
Hilton*. For example. A phenomenal success –

Tracy A commercial flop.

Ray *Artistically.* And take that track on it –

Tracy No individual tracks on the album –

Ray Or *moment* rather …

Tracy Very, very loud and boring this review says.

Ray In which you were trying to say, loudly and clearly,
something about –

Tracy This guy says no sane person could have a clue about what the fuck it is all about –

Ray Something not easily explicable … sure Dave, sure, sure, sure … I am glad you feel I understand Dave, just talk and I'll listen … (*Puts his hand over the mouthpiece.*) Harry?

Harry Still engaged. (*moves towards Ray*) Ray – if I told you they weren't rumours. About pulling the show …

Ray looks up briefly. He simply does not hear what Harry has said.

Ray Do I hear another voice there in the car with you Dave … ? There is someone there with you … ? That's great Dave … oh and *they're on your mobile telephone* … that's great they … they … she's called Lindy … and she *works for your agent* … that's great Dave is she calling your agent, is she calling Peter … ?

Tracy Mum … OK read it.

Ray (*to Harry*) Call the agent.

Harry I can't.

Ray You can, you will and you must.

Harry There is no point.

Ray What is with you? You come in here, you talk rubbish, you say something about a son we never knew you had, you say there are some crazy rumours about the show, none of it makes sense Harry, does it?

Tracy Ray –

Ray What?

Tracy Nothing.

Ray I'm working. Maclellan's working. What do you

want Harry? Maclellan's after another job, did you know? Did you hear that rumour? Her mother reads her big-deal letters from London Weekend, did you hear?

Tracy, during this, has been listening to her mother. As she has been hunting for Ray's information her mum has been reading her the letter. She doesn't betray any sign of reacting to it.

Tracy That's fine Mother, that's fine, that's all I wanted to know ... I just wanted to hear it Mother ... Mother *shut up will you? OK ... ?* Thank you, thank you ... I'll call you later ...

Ray, who has caught this, flashes her a quick, worried look.

Ray What's up Maclellan?

Tracy Nothing's up. Nothing's up.

Ray That's good then. (*to his phone*) She's phoning your agent, that's great Dave ... but he's engaged I see ... (*to Tracy*) Tracy you try the mobile. Soon as the bitch takes her finger off of the dial get on the line and get her out of that car.

Tracy How?

Ray I don't know. Use a Welsh accent. Shout at her. Why ask me. Harry phone the agent.

Harry Why?

Ray We do not want the agent to talk to Hewitt and he has his person in the car there with him and he is probably trying to phone even now, I want you to block lines, I want you to get on that phone you spineless cunt and make some fucking calls, do I have to carry you every fucking step of the way? (*back to his Hewitt phone, all pleasantness*) No, I'm still here Dave. I was listening with great interest to what you had to say there ... and ... sure, sure, sure ... look I do have something specific to ask you but right now I am just enjoying sharing things with you like –

Tracy He's a Pisces.

Ray Star signs ... I'm a Pisces as it happens ... I do not *believe* it, this is amazing Dave ...

Tracy is dialling the mobile as she feeds Ray with stuff.

Harry move your fingers to the fucking dial! The agent. Didn't I say? Block his calls. Stop him getting through to Hewitt.

Harry Ray – how can I spell this out to you? How can I make this clear to you? Do you ever listen to anything anyone ever says to you?

Ray You were born in the year of the rat?

Tracy I'm through! Hullo ... ? Hullo is that Lindy? (*She has assumed a Welsh accent.*) Lindy, it's Bronwen Hughes here from Charing Cross Hospital. I am afraid I have some very bad news for you, your family has been involved in a very serious accident ... all of them ... your mother and father are ... in Tunisia yes, thank God, so they have been spared ... I really can't say over the phone Lindy except that your sister is not expected to last very long ...

Ray I didn't catch that Dave ... you sound as if you are travelling at great speed...

Tracy Yes, it *was* the boiler Lindy, it was the boiler ... had you thought something would go wrong with the boiler ... ? Indeed well it did, it did, it exploded Lindy, it blew up in a quite spectacular fashion ... (*She is looking down the article.*) He is very superstitious.

Harry I am on the phone. Who am I calling?

Tracy Hewitt's agent.

Ray Whatever you do Dave take care because the horoscope for Pisceans today says we are on no account to go near any *hospitals* … I don't believe it … the woman in the car with you has just had a call telling her to go to *Charing Cross Hospital*, my God Dave, I am not … I believe in the Devil, I believe in the Antichrist Dave … I think messages come through all the time … *get her out of the car Dave* …

Harry Hullo, this is Harry Harrod … (*He looks at the phone.*) They hung up.

Ray Dial again.

Tracy Lindy, if he is saying that, give him the phone and get out of the car don't … what was that, I didn't say *hit him with the phone* I said give him the …

Ray You've got the mobile off her Dave, yes but you are not on hands-free Dave, right? Dave can I say something, *you should not* talk on two mobile phones at once while driving Dave, *Dave are you OK?* Dave you cannot steer with your teeth Dave *stop the car Dave please* …   you've stopped, that is good Dave, that is better Dave … She's screaming and she won't get out … ? Wah! Talk to the person on your other mobile Dave … (*to Tracy*) Get her out!

Tracy is through to Hewitt.

Tracy I've got Hewitt. Who am I?

Harry Tracy are you really after another job?

During this speech Tracy has psyched herself up to give a sensational performance as a Chinese doctor.

Tracy Ah hurroh! ... Mistah Hewitt ... ? I am Dr Wong of the Meadway Clinic we have reason to believe you have a Miss Lindy ... Jones, yes, in the car with you ... She is very, very dangerous ... Mistah Hewitt get her out of the car *as soon as possible* ... if necessary use force Mistah Hewitt ... yes Mistah Hewitt.

Both she and Ray wince. Tracy looks at the research article. There is clearly much violence at the other end of the line.

Tracy He once tried to strangle his drummer apparently ...

They both listen. Harry has been dialling.

Harry Hullo this is the Sunlight Laundry ... sure ... it's Harry Harrod sure ... I can't do voices ... look I wanted to say, I wanted to say I was sorry about ... it wasn't my idea, it ...

Ray Don't be too hard on her Dave!

Harry They hung up.

Ray She's out of the car, that's good Dave, that is excellent, just drive, put as much distance between you and her as possible, you and I have to talk Dave ... what do you mean you want to talk to Dr Wong, who is Dr Wong ... ? She is on your mobile, I see, well Dave I want you to talk to me not Dr Wong ...

Tracy He likes Wong.

Ray Excuse me – I am the one winning his confidence here. Where is the percentage in his taking a shine to a Chinese doctor from some private loony bin?

Tracy She is not just any old doctor Ray ... (*She is listening to Hewitt who is clearly rambling on to her.*) There's something about Wong he likes ...

Ray Wong, Wong, Wong, Wong, you are uncontrollable today Maclellan, he needs to talk to *me* not Wong Wong Wong … What was in that letter?

Tracy (*covers the mouthpiece*) He says I have a sympathetic voice. He wants to know how old I am.

Ray Dave, Dave are you there?

Tracy Yes. I twenty-five …

Harry My son is twenty-two …

Ray Great. Good for him. Does he want to be on the show? Does he have a story to tell? And if so what is it? (*to his phone*) Talk to me Dave I need to talk to you.

Harry He has AIDS.

Ray That's really dull Harry. That's really, really dull. Every week you open the papers and there's someone with AIDS. And they're all thin and have videotapes of themselves passing out and they have these *picky* funerals and I think it's dull don't you Maclellan?

Tracy AIDS is dull. It's a switch off. It's breast cancer. That's the thing. That's the disease. (*to her Hewitt phone, as Wong*) You sound as if you have many, many problems Mr Hewitt. In my opinion you need qualified help.

Ray Dave we need to talk …

Harry He has AIDS. I never even knew I had a son you know? This was a woman who … I never knew …

Tracy Ah! Mr Hewitt …

Harry This was a woman who was on the show and … I never even *knew*. You know? I never even knew he was there.

Tracy Ah!

Harry And then he pitches up and tells me he's dying. Can you beat that? I didn't know he existed let alone he was a …

Tracy Yes, yes …

Ray shoots Harry a quick glance. One of those very swift ones that tell you that he is taking all this very seriously. He gives up, for the moment anyway, on Dave.

Ray So he's a you-know-what.

Harry He's a you-know-what.

Tracy I am just fetch our senior psychiatrist who deals with bereavement … if anyone can help you with the death of your dog it is … ah Professor Iliutkin!

Ray gives her a sharp glance.

Ray Professor what?

Tracy Professor who isn't Chinese. I cannot do any more Chinese.

Ray What was it made you go for Chinese? (*He senses his chance to talk to Dave and shouts down his phone.*) Dave can you talk to me now Dave? (*But he doesn't get a response. He rounds on Harry.*) And he has AIDS so he will die and you have to come to terms with it and wear one of those red ribbons at the funeral and become pals with all these faggots for two weeks and pretend you are the father they never had, is that the story? (*with real contempt*) Never mind this boy dying. Maybe you should have noticed him before he got sick? (*a sharp look at him*) You're taking his calls? You are looking after him, right?

Tracy (*on the line to Dave again, this time a Russian*) Hullo Hewitt, here is Professor Iliutkin, doctor of psychiatry specializing in problems of bereavement, you wish to talk to me about Mufty, yes … ? Yes, yes, is dog I know …

Harry Ray do you feel anything at all?

Ray I am completely without human feeling Harry. For some people it was Vietnam. For others it was the collapse of communism. For me it was working on a chat show for twenty years with a spineless cunt who rolled over and died when the fucking bosses decided to push his show later and later and then pulled his staff and then called him a *cunt* and finally pulled his fucking show without him fighting for it.

Tracy (*as Iliutkin*) It was terminal?

Ray And you'll be OK won't you? Mr Anglo-Saxon graduate with shares, and friends on the sixth floor, you'll roll with the punches won't you, they'll 'find something for you' won't they?

Tracy Mr Hewitt, I appreciate that death of dog is a serious matter, I myself have labrador named … er … Tolstoy and I love him. Are you sniffing Hewitt? Vot are you sniffing Hewitt? (*covers phone*) I think he's coked up to the eyeballs …

Ray Why won't he talk to me? What's wrong with Ray Goodenough all of a sudden? (*He strains his ears but doesn't like what he hears.*)

Tracy He loves Iliutkin as well. He loved Wong and he loves Iliutkin. It's my voice or something.

Ray So you're having telephone sex. I must get to talk to him Maclellan. Hasn't he got another mobile phone? Could you get him to a call box and I could ring in?

Tracy Dave … Dave … are you hearink me? Where are you going Hewitt … ? You are going to agent? To *agent*? Hewitt I think … (*She puts her hand over the phone.*)

He's going to his agent.

Ray hasn't really heard the news about the agent. But now he takes it in. Total panic.

Ray Do not let him go anywhere near his agent.

Tracy What do I do?

Ray You talk to him. You talk to people. That's how you persuade them.

Tracy What do I say?

Ray You tell him to go somewhere else.

Tracy To where do I persuade him to go?

Ray You persuade him to go to the *Harry Harrod Show* of course.

Tracy Can you tell me why a Russian psychiatrist specializing in human and animal bereavement should want to persuade a total stranger to go on the *Harry Harrod Show*?

Ray You're a researcher. Use ingenuity.

Tracy Oh this is extraordinary coincidence David, an old friend of mine is just walkink in entitle Ray Goodenough who is, as it happens, from *Harry Harrod Show* ...

Ray Dave this is extraordinary ... this is *weird* Dave, this is the weirdest thing I ever did see in my entire life ... I walk into the *Meadway Clinic* and who do I see but my old friend *Professor Iliutkin* and it turns out she has been talking to you, this is weird, it is weird, it is ... (*to Tracy with some bitterness*) completely unbelievable if you ask me, couldn't you deal with this? Couldn't you work the conversation round from wheat production in Novosibirsk to the *Harry Harrod Show*. I said 'ingenuity'. (*to Dave*) Incredible sure, but that is how it is Dave ... (*to*

Tracy) He wants to talk to you. He wants to know what you're wearing. (*to phone*) Professor Iliutkin is wearing a … a white coat Dave and er … leather boots Dave. Talk to her. She won't go away!

Tracy Hullo Dave!

Ray Yes she's here and the team … full … er … psychiatric team is here too Dave … (*a panic*) There is no need to come here … no need to come to the clinic … I'm headed back to the office … but I could meet you back at the offices whenever suited you … now is fine Dave. You know where it is. I'm on my way … (*He does walking routine.*) Oh, if you wanted Professor Iliutkin to come along I am sure she would, I will talk with her … Professor.

Tracy Oh yes?

Ray How about popping along to the *Harry Harrod Show* with me … (*under his breath*) You can look Russian Maclellan, can't you?

Tracy Da.

Ray (*to phone*) As you can probably hear I am walking down the corridor now Dave, with the professor, with Professor Iliutkin herself Dave, we are … going through the lobby we are … (*motioning to the others to imitate him*) marching through the lobby here, busy lobby … into the er … car park … (*calling to Tracy*) Where's the car Professor? Over there? (*to Dave, very solicitous and chummy*) You'll be able to meet with Harry himself Dave, he'll be down at the offices, he is often there …

Harry Will we ever forget those offices? Will we ever really not be part of all this?

Ray You'd like to meet Harry … sure …

Harry Hi Dave!

Ray Hey, there he is, how extraordinary to find *Harry Harrod* in the *car park* of the *Meadway Clinic*, that is what I call a *coincidence* Dave, yes apparently he has a *brother* who is coming here for treatment, yes we all need treatment Dave, my God we do … (*to Harry for Dave's benefit*) Would you like a lift back to the offices, Harry? (*to Dave*) Just getting into the car now Dave and preparing to drive down to the offices of the *Harry Harrod Show* which are quite close as it happens … (*makes car noises*) He wants to talk to you Professor. He wants to talk.

> *Tracy grabs the phone. Totally in character.*

Tracy I will talk Goodenough. I will discuss with Hewitt. (*She Iliutkins down the phone at Dave.*) Hewitt, yes I too feel great sympathy for you and I am woman Hewitt, with many problems … well Hewitt … you want to know why, you must to come on *Herry Herrod Show*, Hewitt I will tell you I am born in little willage in Russia with unpronounceable name and in willage, yes Hewitt, is little Jew, you understand, by name Plotnik, yes is patronymic Hewitt, is very, very small with large nose and is superficially, vell basically unattractive Hewitt, and I become inwolve with heem and share in his dreams and ve are becomink lovers Hewitt, in his arms I discover the world.

Ray Maclellan –

Tracy Now I am leavink for England Hewitt and do not see Plotnik who is perhaps swept away in pogrom but then in England one night I am turning on television and am very moved by programme which is in fact *Herry Herrod Show* on which is man with, vell basically, severed penis …

Harry Turn left here Ray! Turn left into the main road!

Ray Maclellan –

Tracy Producer of show is calling self Goodenough on credits, Hewitt. I write to heem and discover that this Goodenough is in fact Plotnik. Yes Hewitt he has swum Baltic and escaped regime and put self through night school and become success in TV and I am so proud of him Hewitt he is not an educated man, but he has made something of himself. Many people say is vulgar man and not good but I love him Hewitt and find in him true nobility. Which, Hewitt, is only found in the gutter. And this is why you must come on show. And we must go to *Herry Herrod Show* we will work Hewitt, we must work, for that is all there is Hewitt, we must go to Moscow Hewitt, we must work with Plotnik alongside us Hewitt! I am in mornink for my life.

> *Ray is doing car noises. Pushes her in the back and grabs phone off her.*

Ray Dave? Dave? Did you get that Dave? Are you still there Dave? (*He covers the mouthpiece. To Tracy*) Are you out of your mind Maclellan? Do you want this guy to come on the show? Or do you want him to call the police and have you sectioned under the Mental Health Act? What is with this Plotnik stuff Maclellan? Can we cut out the kissy kissy? Please? Do you expect him to *believe* that? (*back to Dave*) I am glad you were touched by what she said Dave, yes it is true, originally my family name was Plotnik but in television you know the name is important, yes we were lovers Dave, but we are no longer Dave … pressure Dave … pressure of the job … maybe we should have remained lovers Dave, I don't know, I am glad you care about us and want to see us happy Dave – (*to Tracy*) This guy believes everything you tell him. He is a producer's dream Maclellan. (*to Dave*) Well we're just coming up to the building now Dave and … (*breaks off,* *as to an imaginary doorman*) How are you Charlie? Wife and kids all right? Good. Any messages for me? Good. The show is fine, the show is great, sure, sure ... see you Charlie ... (*to Dave*) Charlie. Been on the door as long as I've been in the place. Well it is Dave, it isn't the cold-hearted parody of showbiz you see on the movies, it's like a family really ... (*Breaks off to talk to imaginary friend.*) Hi Stella, how's the cookery programme? All right? Ratings good? *Good!* That is good! (*to Dave*) Stella. She does our cookery programme. (*Does walking. Mimes to the others to do the same.*) Walking along the corridor Dave here and ... sure you want to talk to Harry, talk to Harry, he is right here beside me ... (*Motioning Harry frantically to come over and walk by him.*) I'll give you Harry ... (*Pushes the phone at Harry.*)

Harry Hi ... hi ... no, no, no ... no I am glad ... well I couldn't sound worse than I do on television could I ... ? No, no, no, I am very very well and very very keen for you to come on the show on the 25th ... and I think it would be great if you came right on up to the offices and joined us ... oh sure we are busy ... but, but ... you know ...

Ray does a lot of banging of desks and calling.

Ray Hi Lorraine, hi Pete, hi Fiona, hi James!

Harry Ray's just saying hullo to the team ... they may not all be here when you ... arrive (*Ray has instructed him on this.*) ... cheerio Fiona, see you Pete, bye James ... they're all just off out getting new stories and working on the show. Well park the car, it is right across the street from there Dave, all you have to do is walk in that big blue door and up in the lift and ... (*deep breath*) I'll be honest with you ... I think I've behaved badly and let people down and I haven't fought for things I believe in, but because of today, and you know, Ray, I'm going to try and be better Dave ... you too ... ? You too ... ? *This is*

85

what the show is like Dave … this is what it should be like, just people talking to each other and learning from each other and we've somehow forgotten that there's more talk than ever before Dave, but not good talk and we've got to try and have *good talk* Dave, you know? Sure … sure … like this … well we're both … we're both going to try right? (*Puts his hand over the phone.*) Shouldn't the phones be going?

Ray Maclellan. Dial.

Tracy Dial who?

Ray Dial yourself.

Tracy Dial yourself yourself.

Ray I will. We all should dial ourselves. Keep busy. Dial. Go with this Harry. Go with this. Talk to the guy. Bond with him.

And he is dialling. Another phone in the office goes. Harry talks to Dave.

Harry Sure Dave, sure, I think you were right to … just keep walking Dave, keep on walking right across the street …

Phones are ringing all over the office.

As you can hear Dave it's quite busy here … I better get that Dave … (*to another phone*) Harry Harrod here – just give me two minutes … (*to Dave again*) If you want to know why you should come on the *Harry Harrod Show* you talk to Ray … well we met nearly twenty years ago Dave, and I would never dare say this to his face, but I love the guy …

Ray Too right you wouldn't asshole …

Harry I do, I love the guy … I don't know why Dave, but

because he really does love what he does …

Tracy All the phones are engaged. We are calling our-selves on all lines …

Harry I am going to be better Dave, I am going to … *the point of talking to people like me is that we are no different from anyone else, the point is in the talking Dave, the talking and the trying* … I am going to fight for this show Dave for Ray and for Tracy and … yes for Professor Iliutkin too, she is a remarkable woman … who's Tracy? She's er … out at the moment but she'll be back when Professor Iliutkin goes, she is her twin sister in fact Dave, it's a long story but she is a decent person and I am going in to bat for her and for Ray and for you Dave … sure we will phone down and tell them to send you up …

Ray Hullo … (*He has liberated a phone.*) Hullo this is Ray Goodenough here on the *Harry Harrod Show*, is there a Mr Dave Hewitt there … ? There is, that is great, could you send him up please, sure … shall I have a word with him … (*to Dave*) Hi Dave this is Ray … I'll talk you through it on the mobile Dave, I'll tell you just where to go, sure he is right here, I will take the phone from him … (*covers the mouthpiece*) before he starts *crying* and telling me how he has wanted to *suck my cock* for all these years but has always been afraid to ask.

Harry Ray listen –

Ray No you listen –

Harry Tracy – what was in that letter your mother … are you really going for another job?

Tracy It was from the doctor. The cancer's spread.

Ray It's *what?*

Tracy It's spread. To the bones.

Ray You *what?*

Tracy Don't start getting sloppy with me Mr Goodenough. Please. It doesn't suit you.

Ray Tracy – my dear –

Tracy Can we just get on and do some fucking work?

Ray (*to Dave*) I am taking the phone from him now Dave and … you hear me, good … good, good, that is good … look walk straight ahead of you and when you get to the lifts press five, fifth floor … I'll tell you why you should come on the *Harry Harrod Show*, I'll tell you why you … I'll tell you about me, sure, sure I feel we've got to know each other well enough that I don't want to bullshit you any more because I spend my *life* bullshitting, Dave, that is what I do twenty-four hours a day, it's bullshit, bullshit, bullshit, that is how I make my living and I sometimes no longer know what is real and what is false and what I feel and what I don't feel … well they're a commodity to me Dave, I deal in them, I deal in people's feelings … right go out of the lift and turn left, do you see a long, long corridor in front of you … you do? You do … ? That's good Dave, start to walk down it … now don't jack out on me now will you Dave because I am telling you the truth now, I am telling you the truth of my heart … sure, sure, about me … well the truth about me and the truth about why you should come on to the show Dave are one and the same because I am the damn show Dave … I am it … I am the one who makes the calls and plans the schedules and lies awake at night and sweats blood and eats and sleeps and dreams it I do … I eat and I drink the *Harry Harrod Show* … it is my constant companion Dave, and do you know why Dave, I am going to tell you the truth now and not this bullshit about love and how we all are one big family, that is bullshit Dave, and you know it is bullshit, of course you do … don't give up on me Dave, keep walking, don't give up on me –

Tracy Ray –

Ray Did I ask your opinion?

Harry Ray –

Ray Did I ask yours? Did I ever ask yours? Didn't I just get on and *do* it? Did I ask you to bleed all over me?

Harry Ray I'm going to try and –

Ray You're going to try. And what? You're going to try. Harry you've never done shit. You've never kept a single one of your promises to me or anyone else so why should you start now? (*to the phone*) Just keep on going Dave, I know it's a long one but you mustn't stop now, just keep on going, you hear me … well *why* does it mean so much to me Dave, I'll tell you why … because I have fuck all else … I don't believe in anything Dave, I don't believe in love, I don't believe in prayer or art or science or any of that bullshit, I don't … no, no, no … no I don't, I don't … they're dead Dave, the way parents die, you know, and all of that was so much bullshit too Dave … no, no, no, I do not think you understand …

Both Harry and Tracy are watching him. Utterly absorbed in his performance.

… it doesn't mean *anything* to me … it doesn't mean anything more than anything else I do … it's like the next drink or the next gulp of air … and why do I want you, well I just want the next thing the way we all do and although when I want, oh my God how I want it, it's nothing, it's like water condensing on glass or a breath of air gone as quickly as it came, it is nothing Dave, do you see it is of absolutely no significance and yet, how I want it, the way we all want that next breath although we may not even know why we want it any more, we just want

89

want want the next thing, the next touch of a stranger, the next voice, the next new person to walk into the room … you must be right outside Dave … you must be right outside … and I can't hear you Dave … the carpets are really soft and I can't hear you … is that it or are you putting me on Dave, is that it? Are you putting me on Dave, is that it … ? I can't lie to you Dave, I can't give you any stuff about why you should come on in or what any of it means or how or why or when or even if you should say yes to me but that is what I want, that is all there is Dave, what I want … come in Dave, don't put me on, come in Dave …

He waits. Harry and Tracy are turned to the door but no one is coming through it. Ray stays glued to his phone.

Come on in Dave, OK … come in now, come on … don't put me on Dave … say yes Dave, show yourself Dave, be in a room with a person and talk can't you?

Tracy and Harry and he stand with their backs to the audience looking towards the door and waiting and waiting and waiting for someone to come through it to end the silence.
Slow fade.